AFFIRM
(—THE—)
WORD

THE SPIRITUAL PRACTICE OF
SPEAKING & LIVING GOD'S WORD

Compiled by J. Marie Jones

Copyright © 2020 by J. Marie Jones
www.affirmtheword.org

ISBN: 978-1-64953-075-2

Absolute Author
Publishing House

Published by Absolute Author Publishing House
New Orleans, Louisiana

For wholesale inquiries contact: sales@affirmtheword.org
Printed in China

For

The twelve-year-old me discovering God,
the many versions of me that would continue to seek His face in the
years to follow, and all those searching for Him in a real and true way.
May your belief in His existence, and diligence in seeking him, bring you
total healing: Joy unspeakable, peace unexplainable,
and rewards far greater than the mind can comprehend.

Without faith, it is impossible to please God,
for anyone who comes to God must believe that He exists,
and that He rewards those who earnestly seek Him.
Hebrews 11:6

Table of Contents

Biblical Word Affirmations

Preface

Most believers, meaning those who have chosen to follow God's will by making Jesus Christ Lord of their lives, understand that there is power in the Word of God. However, very few understand the importance of speaking the Word of God, as well as life-affirming words over their lives every day. That's right, every day. Why? Because every day we are bombarded with negative words, imagery, experiences, and subsequently feelings that rob us of the joy, peace, and blessings afforded to us under grace as a result of our salvation. Right thinking, living, and being does not come about through osmosis. It is not automatic and requires effort and participation on our part, which starts by first, speaking the change we want to see and be.

Many people, including believers, also fail to understand the importance of speaking life-giving words with faith and intention; they ignorantly speak negativity over themselves and those they love with the full force of their hurt, resentment, and anger. Or, they speak "positive affirmations" with fear and speculation, "hoping" for change, but doubtful that it will come. As a result, they consistently manifest the things they DON'T want in their lives with no clue how to stop the cycle. That is why the name of this book is not merely "Speak The Word" but AFFIRM the Word, which denotes speaking with faith, intention, and full assurance in that which you are speaking. Here's how Dictionary.com defines the word affirm:

Affirm: to state or assert positively; maintain as true: to confirm or ratify: to assert solemnly: to express agreement with or commitment to; uphold; support.

1

In other words, to agree with and declare what you know to be true, of everything you believe and hope to believe, with life-affirming words over yourself, your relationships, and your circumstances, as well as everything else God has Divinely purposed for your life.

People often confuse conversion (instant salvation through one's faith and confession in Jesus Christ), with transformation (gradual, yet consistent change in one's thinking and behavior), as being one and the same. No– real lasting transformation takes WORK, not in our own strength because righteous, sustainable change is not possible in our own strength but through the power of the Holy Spirit, as we internalize God's Word, speak it over our lives without ceasing, and are led by His spirit concerning our life's purpose in the process. Nothing is impossible for the person with a heart surrendered to God's will, and a willingness to be transformed into His image, through His Word. And it is so!

Introduction

Why Affirm The Word?

Proverbs 18:20-21 says: From the fruit of his mouth, a man's belly is filled; with the harvest from his lips, he is satisfied. The tongue has the power of life and death, and those who love it will eat its fruit.

I have been a believer (AKA follower of Christ) since I was 12 years old; however, notice I didn't say, "A practicing believer." Maybe a pretending believer, an ignorant believer, an inconsistent believer, and possibly a number of different types of believers all of us have had the pleasure or misfortune of encountering. But one thing I can truly say about myself is that no matter how off I was in my efforts to follow God, I always maintained a sincere desire to become all that He called me to be. I had no idea exactly how to do that, and until a few years ago, I had no idea where to start to ensure lasting and consistent transformation. But I knew I had to start somewhere.

At the time, I was enduring a serious situation on my job. You guessed it; I'd gotten myself into a terrible work "situationship." I wouldn't dare classify it like that at the time, as it indeed had all the elements of a relationship. But whatever one wants to call it, "it" was not good. However, I couldn't, and quite possibly didn't want to see that at the time. My almost twenty-year marriage had just ended, and after doing things "God's way" most of my life, and being miserable, I was determined to really, once and for all, do things "my way," but with God's help, of course.

Eventually, after many scrapes, bruises, tears, and tantrums, I was beginning to see that I could no longer do things as I had always done. Meaning, I could no longer try to live righteously in my own strength, formulate plans steeped in my own self-interest (yet with a righteous objective), barter with God to bless said plans through sacrificial service, fail miserably, formulate my own methods of rescue and retaliation, fail miserably, beg God for rescue, rinse, and repeat. Even though I'd become more selfish in meeting my direct wants and needs, I was still behaving the same way I did when I was "serving God" because my service had always been about trying to protect myself and secure my future.

Therefore, my usual M.O. of trying to come up with ways of getting out of the situation, pleading and threatening the offender, bartering, consulting friends and family, and soliciting outside intervention, was not an option. Also, Ms. Cleo, the TV Psychic, had passed away and she too was no longer an option, so there wasn't even that last shred of hope in the all too familiar, "Call me now!" – Lol! May she rest in peace.

In all seriousness, I am thankful that during that time, I met a woman who gave me some valuable insights. I'd heard that she had the spiritual gift of knowledge, and although I was not sure that still existed, I wanted to find out for myself. I'd actually met her on Facebook through an old friend, and on learning that she was starting a Brick and Mortar operation and was looking for a graphic designer, I sent her a message that I did logo design. We soon connected, and as we were reviewing her spec sheet, I began to tell her a bit about what was happening with me. I wasn't sharing with her so much about the situation, just where I believe I was going, and where I wanted to be in my spiritual walk. She then began to tell me about all that was happening in my life, the people who were around me during that season, and what she was seeing concerning my walk with the Father and my spiritual gift.

About an hour into our call, I decided that I needed to start recording because I could not believe how accurate she was concerning me — internally. She asked me straight out, "Why won't you commit to fully following God." WOW! I asked her how she knew that. I mean, that was a major question because I had never spoken about my hesitation, but had thought of the specific reasons why many times. It was years before that I'd decided internally that I would not completely turn myself over to God in total surrender. Oh, I believed in Him. I wanted to follow Him so that He would bless me, but I wasn't trying to be a minister or anything. I wasn't trying to be "perfect." Why? Well, the main reasons were: #1) I didn't want to start something I couldn't live out, #2) I didn't want God to ask me to do something I didn't want to do, and #3) I didn't want to become a holy-roller, walking around with opaque stockings and a doily on my head; I'm just keepin' it real! Simply put, I wanted to retain my false sense of control.

She went on to say that angels were telling her this, and she was just simply repeating what they were saying. She then proceeded to tell me what my spiritual gift was, not meaning the practical application but the result of my gifting poured out in service on this earth. She also told me about the supernatural developments that would take place in my life if I finally surrendered myself to God. This included how to do so; surrender, that is. And lastly, she told me about a book that would change my life.

The name of that book was *The Game of Life and How to Play It,* by Florence Schoval Schinn. The name alone had me totally intrigued, and change my life it did. To this date, I have now read and/or listened to it almost 100 times. Not only has it taught me about the power of Christ that lives in all believers, but it also taught me the power of speaking the

Word to manifest change within us, ultimately changing our surroundings, both naturally and spiritually.

The Word of God teaches that there are two critical things believers must do upon conversion. The first is to be transformed into their NEW, Divine selves by renewing their minds. Conversion is free and only requires us to accept and believe. Transformation takes place via the work of the Holy Spirit in us, as we internalize God's Word and renew our mind in the process. The second is to follow Christ. One cannot effectively and consistently do the latter without simultaneously doing the former. We will always be a work in progress. The hope, however, is that our constant evolution is ever toward the image of God and not that of our carnal self.

"And do not be conformed to this world, but be transformed by the renewing of your mind, so that you may prove what the will of God is, that which is good and acceptable and perfect."
Romans 12:2 NASB

Learning to follow Christ at such a young age, I had no idea what I was doing. I didn't know if what I was doing was right, or for the right reasons, or anything. When I did try to research, memorize, and live certain scriptures in the Word, I was told by parents, ministry leaders, and other seasoned "saints" that I was doing too much, and no one really did the word "literally."

I didn't know that I could ask God to reveal Himself to me in a way I could understand and that He would. I didn't know that God means what He says concerning His character and how we are to love and serve Him, either directly or via various teachings throughout His Word. I also didn't know how important it was for ME to speak His work over my life, every day, into my OWN hearing. I always thought the scripture, "Faith comes by hearing, and hearing by the Word of God" (Romans 10:17), meant through the preacher.

I was not encouraged to search the scripture for myself, and during the many times I tried, I would eventually get overwhelmed whenever I hit a "thus," "thither," "beseech," or biblical genealogy full of weird sounding names. I would also be admonished for trying to do too much, or be "perfect," which really discouraged me. Looking back, it would have helped to have key scriptures, in plain English close by, and the understanding of my need to speak them out loud, to help me stay on course. It would have also helped to have certain scriptures or concepts in the bible explained in concise, everyday terms, like, how to really forgive someone or how to cast your burdens on God. Just about everyone I knew seemed to "cast their burdens" on God by getting to the end of their rope, throwing themselves on the altar in desperation, and then getting up from said altar, only to go back to doing the same ol' thing as before, hoping and praying for a different result.

Now, some people would call that insanity, but I call it 'just not knowing any better.' There's a saying that goes, "when you know better, you do better." The purpose of this book is to assist believers endeavoring to be transformed into the image of God, with internalizing God's Word and engaging in the spiritual practice of speaking LIFE, while in pursuit of their Divine purpose. Helping you to know better by providing you with indexed scriptures to easily learn the Word, and do better by putting the Word into practice, through the power and assistance of the Holy Spirit.

In my first attempt at committing scripture to memory, I was directed to a topical concordance. If you know anything about a concordance, then you are aware that they house about 20,000 topics, over 100,000 verses, and are usually as large as those old-school coffee table bibles. Affirm The Word, however, contains a small index of what I believe to be critical scripture verses essential to the believer's walk, for protection against spiritual warfare and assistance with walking in total victory. It is meant to be carried with you daily, and it is spiral bound so that you can quickly reference scripture notations, write and access personal notes, and even tear out a prayer request or two for posting in your prayer closet.

There is no doubt that being created in God's Divine image, we are all worthy and valued as human beings. But, we must surrender our will to His plan in order for that plan to manifest. By consistently and prayerfully engaging in the practice of speaking God's Word over your life as well as the vision birthed in your heart through the Spirit of God, you will be empowered to walk in total trust in His ability to transform you into the highest expression of your true "self."

May the fruit of your efforts bring forth with clarity, your God-ordained purpose in this earth, a purpose He established for your life before time began. And may this book be to you, a pivotal resource to supplement your daily bible reading, prayer time, meditation, and fellowship with our Heavenly Father. For His glory, your good, and the good of others. And it is so!

Biblical Word Affirmations

Affliction

For he has not despised or abhorred the affliction of the afflicted, and he has not hidden his face from him but has heard when he cried to him. Psalm 22:24

The afflicted shall eat and be satisfied; those who seek him shall praise the Lord! May your hearts live forever! Psalm 22:26

When the righteous cry for help, the Lord hears and delivers them out of all their troubles. The Lord is near to the brokenhearted and saves the crushed in spirit. Many are the afflictions of the righteous, but the Lord delivers him out of them all. He keeps all his bones; not one of them is broken. Psalm 34:17-20

It is good for me that I was afflicted, that I might learn your statutes. Psalm 119:71

Not only that, but we rejoice in our sufferings, knowing that suffering produces endurance, and endurance produces character, and character produces hope, and hope does not put us to shame because God's love has been poured into our hearts through the Holy Spirit who has been given to us. Romans 5:3-5

For I consider that the sufferings of this present time are not worth comparing with the glory that is to be revealed to us. Romans 8:18

So we do not lose heart. Though our outer self is wasting away, our inner self is being renewed day by day. For this light momentary affliction is preparing for us an eternal weight of glory beyond all comparison, as we look not to the things that are seen but to the things that are unseen. For the things that are seen are transient, but the things that are unseen are eternal. 2 Corinthians 4:16-18

But he said to me, "My grace is sufficient for you, for my power is made perfect in weakness." Therefore I will boast all the more gladly of my weaknesses, so that the power of Christ may rest upon me. For the sake of Christ, then, I am content with weaknesses, insults, hardships, persecutions, and calamities. For when I am weak, then I am strong. 2 Corinthians 12:9-10

Count it all joy, my brothers, when you meet trials of various kinds, for you know that the testing of your faith produces steadfastness. And let steadfastness have its full effect, that you may be perfect and complete, lacking in nothing. James 1:2-4

Behold, we consider those blessed who remained steadfast. You have heard of the steadfastness of Job, and you have seen the purpose of the Lord, how the Lord is compassionate and merciful. James 5:11

Anger

A fool's anger is known at once, But a prudent man conceals dishonor. Proverbs 12:16 NASB

A quick-tempered man acts foolishly, And a man of evil devices is hated. Proverbs 14:17 NASB

He who is slow to anger has great understanding, But he who is quick-tempered exalts folly. Proverbs 14:29 NASB

A gentle answer turns away wrath, But a harsh word stirs up anger. Proverbs 15:1 NASB

A hot-tempered man stirs up strife, But the slow to anger calms a dispute. Proverbs 15:18 NASB

He who is slow to anger is better than the mighty, And he who rules his spirit, than he who captures a city. Proverbs 16:32 NASB

He who restrains his words has knowledge, And he who has a cool spirit is a man of understanding. Proverbs 17:27 NASB

Good sense makes one slow to anger, and it is his glory to overlook an offense. Proverbs 19:11

A man of great wrath will pay the penalty, for if you deliver him, you will only have to do it again. Proverbs 19:19

Make no friendship with a man given to anger, nor go with a wrathful man . . . Proverbs 22:24

A fool always loses his temper, But a wise man holds it back. Proverbs 29:11 NASB

An angry person stirs up conflict, and a hot-tempered person commits many sins. Proverbs 29:22 NIV

Do not be quickly provoked in your spirit, for anger resides in the lap of fools. Ecclesiastes 7:9 NIV

But I say to you that everyone who is angry with his brother will be liable to judgment; whoever insults his brother will be liable to the council; and whoever says, 'You fool!' will be liable to the hell of fire. Matthew 5:22

Never take your own revenge, beloved, but leave room for the wrath of God, for it is written, "Vengeance is Mine, I will repay," says the Lord. "But if your enemy is hungry, feed him, and if he is thirsty, give him a drink; for in so doing you will heap burning coals on his head." Do not be overcome by evil, but overcome evil with good. Romans 12:19-21 NASB

Be angry and do not sin; do not let the sun go down on your anger, and give no opportunity to the devil. Ephesians 4:26-27

Let all bitterness and wrath and anger and clamor and slander be put away from you, along with all malice. Be kind to one another, tenderhearted, forgiving one another, as God in Christ forgave you. Ephesians 4:31-32

But now you also put them all aside: anger, wrath, malice, slander, and abusive speech from your mouth. Colossians 3:8 NASB

Have nothing to do with foolish, ignorant controversies; you know that they breed quarrels. And the Lord's servant must not be quarrelsome but kind to everyone, able to teach, patiently enduring evil . . . 2 Timothy 2:23-24

For an overseer, as God's steward, must be above reproach. He must not be arrogant or quick-tempered or a drunkard or violent or greedy for gain . . . Titus 1:7

Older men are to be sober-minded, dignified, self-controlled, sound in faith, in love, and in steadfastness. Titus 2:2

Know this, my beloved brothers: let every person be quick to hear, slow to speak, slow to anger; for the anger of man does not produce the righteousness of God. James 1:19-20

Anxiety

Have I not commanded you? Be strong and courageous. Do not be frightened, and do not be dismayed, for the Lord your God is with you wherever you go." Joshua 1:9

"Therefore I tell you, do not be anxious about your life, what you will eat or what you will drink, nor about your body, what you will put on. Is not life more than food, and the body more than clothing? Look at the birds of the air: they neither sow nor reap nor gather into barns, and yet your heavenly Father feeds them. Are you not of more value than they? And which of you by being anxious can add a single hour to his span of life? And why are you anxious about clothing? Consider the lilies of the field, how they grow: they neither toil nor spin, yet I tell you, even Solomon in all his glory was not arrayed like one of these. But if God so clothes the grass of the field, which today is alive and tomorrow is thrown into the oven, will he not much more clothe you, O you of little faith? Therefore do not be anxious, saying, 'What shall we eat?' or 'What shall we drink?' or 'What shall we wear?' For the Gentiles seek after all these things, and your heavenly Father knows that you need them all. Matthew 6:25-32

Do not be anxious about anything, but in everything by prayer and supplication with thanksgiving let your requests be made known to God. And the peace of God, which surpasses all understanding, will guard your hearts and your minds in Christ Jesus. Philippians 4:6-7

"Let not your hearts be troubled. Believe in God; believe also in me. In my Father's house are many rooms. If it were not so, would I have told you that I go to prepare a place for you? And if I go and prepare a place for you, I will come again and will take you to myself, that where I am you may be also. And you know the way to where I am going." John 14:1-4

Peace I leave with you; my peace I give to you. Not as the world gives do I give to you. Let not your hearts be troubled, neither let them be afraid. You heard me say to you, 'I am going away, and I will come to you.' If you loved me, you would have rejoiced, because I am going to the Father, for the Father is greater than I. John 14:27-28

Reflections on Casting Your Burdens

In 1 Peter 5:7, the Word of God encourages us to cast our cares upon God because He cares for us. However, for many years, I struggled to do that, not really knowing how. For example, I would certainly bring a matter to God, but would have no idea how to leave it with Him and still do "my part" to bring about a favorable resolution.

It was not until I read Florence Scovel Shinn's *The Game of Life and How To Play It,* that I began to understand how to actually put "casting the burden" upon God into practice. In it, she gives an example of a woman who was to be given a piano, but it was required of her to remove the one currently sitting in her home before she could receive the new one. With the new piano on its way, it came to her to repeat, "I cast this burden on the Christ within, and I go free." A few moments later, her phone rang. It was a friend asking if she could rent her old piano, and it was moved out a few minutes before the new one arrived.

It was after reading this story that I began to practice repeating this affirmation, coupled with other scriptures concerning asking, and of course, 1 Peter 5:7. Not only has engaging in this practice brought about tremendous manifestations of God's supernatural intervention in my life, but it has also enabled me to remain at peace and maintain full assurance in God's ability to intervene on my behalf in the process. I was also relieved from engaging in truly toxic habits like calling people to continuously discuss the problem and/or feverishly trying to come up with ways to resolve the issue myself, even though I "gave it to God."

Since learning how to cast my cares upon God, there have been too many instances of God's power showing up for me to list. However, I wanted to reflect on this topic in particular so that others might be encouraged in their efforts to bring issues to God and truly wait for him to provide a complete and unequivocal resolution. God doesn't need our assistance in "figuring things out." He already knows how He will, and is already assisting you, and He will do so to the degree that you surrender the matter to Him.

If you trust him to get you to the door, but not through it, can you really blame Him if you decide to kick it in when you arrive, causing all hell to break loose? Granted, God always knows what we are going to do before we do it. He is merciful and kind, but we are still subject to the consequences of our actions when we take matters into our own hands.

When facing a matter, from the smallest issue to the greatest circumstance, I encourage you to truly cast your burden on God, by FIRST, bringing it to Him in prayer, NOT, after you've done all you could do. I then encourage you to continue thanking Him for His supernatural intervention, and in moments of doubt, speak his Word over the matter, starting with 1 Peter 5:7, and other scriptures in this book concerning asking and faith. This should be done whenever the matter comes to mind or whenever any information contrary to God's favorable and perfect resolution presents itself.

If you've already told someone about the matter, the only follow-up you need to give is that you've cast the burden on God and that you are awaiting His resolution. That's it. There's no need to discuss details, how you're feeling (unless overjoyed with expectation), or vent. God has it, so it's already done. Therefore your words, actions, and disposition should reflect that at all times. And in moments when you are tempted to take matters into your own hands, continue to speak and believe that God's perfect resolution is on its way, in His time.
And it is so!

Asking

Delight yourself in the Lord, and he will give you the desires of your heart. Psalm 37:4

Call to me and I will answer you, and will tell you great and hidden things that you have not known. Jeremiah 33:3

"Ask, and it will be given to you; seek, and you will find; knock, and it will be opened to you. For everyone who asks receives, and the one who seeks finds, and to the one who knocks it will be opened. Matthew 7:7-8

Again I say to you, if two of you agree on earth about anything they ask, it will be done for them by my Father in heaven. Matthew 18:19

And Jesus said to him, "'If you can'! All things are possible for one who believes." Mark 9:23

Therefore I tell you, whatever you ask in prayer, believe that you have received it, and it will be yours. Mark 11:24

If you abide in me, and my words abide in you, ask whatever you wish, and it will be done for you. John 15:7

In that day you will ask nothing of me. Truly, truly, I say to you, whatever you ask of the Father in my name, he will give it to you. Until now you have asked nothing in my name. Ask, and you will receive, that your joy may be full. John 16:23-24

Do not be anxious about anything, but in everything by prayer and supplication with thanksgiving let your requests be made known to God. And the peace of God, which surpasses all understanding, will guard your hearts and your minds in Christ Jesus. Philippians 4:6-7

Let us then with confidence draw near to the throne of grace, that we may receive mercy and find grace to help in time of need. Hebrews 4:16

If any of you lacks wisdom, let him ask God, who gives generously to all without reproach, and it will be given him. James 1:5

You ask and do not receive, because you ask wrongly, to spend it on your passions. James 4:3

And whatever we ask we receive from him, because we keep his commandments and do what pleases him. 1 John 3:22

And this is the confidence that we have toward him, that if we ask anything according to his will he hears us. And if we know that he hears us in whatever we ask, we know that we have the requests that we have asked of him. 1 John 5:14-15

Belief/Unbelief

"You are my witnesses," declares the LORD, and my servant whom I have chosen, so that you may know and believe me and understand that I am he. Before me no god was formed, nor will there be one after me. Isaiah 43:10

But whoever causes one of these little ones who believe in me to sin, it would be better for him to have a great millstone fastened around his neck and to be drowned in the depth of the sea. Matthew 18:6

And Jesus said to him, "'If You can?' All things are possible to him who believes." Mark 9:23 NASB

Whoever believes in him is not condemned, but whoever does not believe is condemned already, because he has not believed in the name of the only Son of God. John 3:18

Do not let your hearts be troubled. You believe in God; believe also in me. John 14:1

But these are written so that you may believe that Jesus is the Christ, the Son of God, and that by believing you may have life in his name. John 20:31

I pray that the eyes of your heart may be enlightened, so that you will know what is the hope of His calling, what are the riches of the glory of His inheritance in the saints, and what is the surpassing greatness of His power toward us who believe. These are in accordance with the working of the strength of His might. Ephesians 1:18-19 NASB

And we also thank God constantly for this, that when you received the word of God, which you heard from us, you accepted it not as the word of men but as what it really is, the word of God, which is at work in you believers. 1 Thessalonians 2:13

For to this end we toil and strive, because we have our hope set on the living God, who is the Savior of all people, especially of those who believe.1 Timothy 4:10

Though you have not seen him, you love him. Though you do not now see him, you believe in him and rejoice with joy that is inexpressible and filled with glory, obtaining the outcome of your faith, the salvation of your souls.1 Peter 1:8-9

Affirmations for Supernatural Belief

I believe in God. He loves me, and I love Him. He is my Father, and He and I are one. Therefore, I reflect His love, life, and light – everywhere I go – in everything I say and do.

I am only influenced by positive beliefs and thoughts.

I am Who God says I am; blessed and appropriately equipped to fulfill my Divine purpose in the earth. I am that which I believe I am.

I am filled with positive expectations.

I am the master of my beliefs and attitudes.

I have complete confidence that God is my instant, constant, and abundant supply.

I believe that I can do all things through the power of Christ within.

Reflections on Binding and Loosing
With commentary from bindingandloosing.com

Truly I say to you, whatever you bind on earth shall have been bound in heaven; and whatever you loose on earth shall have been loosed in heaven. Matthew 18:18 NASB

This topic was one of the hardest for me to research. I've actually been trying to understand it's meaning and how to apply it practically in my everyday living for years, albeit, always with a hint of doubt concerning whether or not I was doing "it" properly. While conducting an online search, one will encounter a number of differing opinions as to what Binding and Loosing actually is, and how to do "it".

The Greek scholar, A. T. Robertson, wrote about binding and loosing: "To 'bind' (dêsêis) in rabbinical language is to forbid; to 'loose' (lusêis) is to permit" [emphasis ours].

Therefore, a better translation of this verse would be:

(Matthew 16:19 International Standard Version, good understandable translation) "I will give you the keys to the kingdom of heaven. Whatever you *prohibit* on earth will have been *prohibited* in heaven, and whatever you *permit* on earth will have been *permitted* in heaven."

This is a topic that can go quite deep and extend for quite some time. Therefore, I've enlisted my friends at bindingandloosing.com (yes,

21

there is a whole entire section of their website dedicated to this) to give us a summary of their exhaustive research on the topic of Binding and Loosing.

Their research, which cites *numerous* commentaries, defines the kingdom of heaven to be that of the true Church on earth, the house of God where the Gospel will come, of which Peter is the steward bearing the keys. The fact that Jesus gave Simon Peter the keys of the kingdom of heaven first means that Peter would be used to open the door of faith to the world, the first to preach the gospel to both Jews and Gentiles. Peter made a confession that Jesus was the Messiah, the Son of the living God. His confession of the Divinity of our Lord was the first made by man. Therefore, Peter was given the keys of the kingdom of heaven (i.e., God chose him among all the apostles), that Gentiles should first hear the Word of the Gospel and believe. All this assumes, that Peter's use of the keys will be in accordance with the teaching and mind of Christ.

Peter first opened the kingdom of heaven to the Gentiles when he preached to Cornelius at Cæsarea. Peter also opened the kingdom of heaven in his sermon at The Great Pentecost. It is important to note that while Peter took the lead, the keys were later given to all the apostles and to no other mortal. This promise was first made to Simon Peter (Matthew 16:19) and then to the other apostles (Matthew 18:18), and cannot be understood as extending to all Christians or ministers.

Now, as for those that teach that binding or loosing applies to demons or Satan, it should also be noted that binding and loosing does not refer to persons, but to things - "whatsoever," not whosoever. It refers to rites and ceremonies in the Church. Among the Jews, binding and loosing means forbidding and allowing. And so as directed by the Holy Spirit, whatever they bound, that is, declared forbidden and

22

unlawful, was just that, and that which they loosed, that is, declared lawful and free for use, remained so. Accordingly, they bound some things, which before were loosed, and loosed some things, which before were bound.

For instance, they prohibited or declared unlawful the act of circumcision, which after the death of Christ, they declared to be no longer of use as circumcision is now that of the heart and not the flesh. (Romans 2:28-29). They bound or forbade the observance of days, months, times, and years; (i.e., the keeping of the various ceremonial holy feast days, new moons, and ceremonial Sabbaths), which were only for the Jews. This included the first day of the New Year, and of every month, the Day of Atonement, Passover, Pentecost, Tabernacles, the Jubilee year, and ceremonial sabbatical years (Galatians 4:9-10). See Colossians 2:16 for more on this. These days did not include the Sabbath of the Lord, which is one of the Ten Commandments. They loosed or declared lawful and free both civil and religious conversation between Jews and Gentiles, whereas before the Jews had no dealings with the Gentiles. They would not enter their houses, or keep company, have a conversation, or eat and drink with them. But now, it was determined and declared that no man should be called common or unclean and that in Christ Jesus and in his Church, there is no distinction as Jew or Gentile (Acts 10:28). These things now by them, being bound or loosed, pronounced unlawful or lawful, were confirmed as such by the authority of God, and are likewise to be considered the same by us.

It was clear and commonly understood by the Jews at that time that binding signified a declaration for anything that was unlawful to do, and loosing signified, on the contrary, a declaration of something as lawful. Our Savior spoke to his disciples in a language that they understood, so that they were not in the least at a loss to comprehend what he meant. The fact that it may not be clear to us is no reason why we should conclude that it was obscure to them. Also, these phrases of binding and loosing occur nowhere else in the New Testament other than in Matthew, who is supposed to have written his Gospel first in Hebrew, before it was then translated into Greek.

Today, many Christians fearlessly overstep their bounds and go "where angels fear to tread." *Some* Christians, with overstated power and authority, do what even the archangel Michael dared not do. Man's verbal barrages do not disturb Satan, but they do displease God. Those who would use extra-biblical spiritual warfare techniques to place themselves in rulership over principalities and powers in the heavenly places are taking over God's rightful place of authority.

The false teachers described by Peter and Jude took it upon themselves to do this, and God's Word rebukes them for it: "…These false teachers are bold and arrogant, and show no respect for the glorious beings above; instead, they insult them. Even the angels, who are so much stronger and mightier than these false teachers, do not accuse them with insults in the presence of the Lord." (2 Peter 2:10-11 GNB). This warning is repeated in Jude 1:8-9 GNB, "Not even the archangel Michael did this. In his quarrel with the Devil, when they argued about who would have the body of Moses, Michael did not dare condemn the Devil with insulting words, but said, The Lord rebuke you!" We also find in Zechariah 3:2 GNB, "The angel of the LORD said to Satan, May the LORD condemn you, Satan!"; an angel would not rebuke Satan but left it to the person who had the authority.

The response of some spiritual warfare teachers to these scriptures has been, "Yes, but we are higher than the angels, the angels cannot do this, but we can." Yet, Hebrews 2:6-7 GNB says, "Instead, as it is said somewhere in the Scriptures: "What are human beings, O God, that you should think of them; mere human beings, that you should care for them? You made them for a little while lower than the angels; you crowned them with glory and honor." Saying we are higher than the angels ignores the clear teachings of the passages in Jude and 2 Peter. Jude clearly states that those who revile angelic majesties are wrong for doing so, and if the archangel Michael did not dare do this, even more, should we refrain from doing so.

So, what does the Bible teach in regard to spiritual warfare? James explains the basic manner in which this should be done. Do not miss that there are two steps to be followed here. The first and very important step is to submit yourself to God in every way, and the second is to resist the enemy, and he will eventually flee (James 4:7). There is a reflection on this very topic involving the practical application of The Whole Armor of God, which must be worn and activated through prayer, in order to successfully stand against spiritual warfare.

There are times when a believer may not be strong enough in their faith to resist the enemy on their own. An unbeliever is also powerless to fight against spiritual warfare, as they have not been filled with the Holy Spirit and thus power to withstand the enemy. Therefore, I think it's important to note two scriptures that speak to the authority of the believer, and our ability to overcome the enemy and satanic forces on another's behalf, through the power of Christ.

Truly, truly, I say to you, he who believes in Me, the works that I do, he will do also; and greater works than these he will do; because I go to the Father. John 14:12 NASB

25

Behold, I have given you authority to tread on serpents and scorpions, and over all the power of the enemy, and nothing will injure you.
Luke 10:19 NASB

Therefore, confess your sins to one another, and pray for one another so that you may be healed. The effective prayer of a righteous man can accomplish much. James 5:16 NASB

These verses speak to the authority that the believer has been given to actively engage the enemy and his forces, when empowered by the Spirit of Christ. However, our primary instruction to stand against spiritual warfare is to RESIST the devil and his forces, and he will flee. Attempting to engage the enemy in any other way should only take place through the direct leading of God. But– it should be noted that this level of spiritual warfare is NOT for the novice believer, and is case-by-case through the leading of the Holy Spirit.

You must be clearly, and unequivocally lead by God to engage in direct confrontation (i.e. casting out demons), with the enemy and his forces. There are entire books on this subject alone, and I am not equipped to give you a breakdown of how to do that, so I won't. Nevertheless, I pray you take the time to meditate on the aforementioned scriptures, those below, and others you may find during your personal bible study on this topic. God has given us the power and authority to overcome the enemy and the forces of this world, but you can only mount your defense by equipping yourself with His amour– for His glory, your good, and the good of others. And it is so!

Binding and Loosing

I will give you the keys of the kingdom of heaven, and whatever you bind on earth shall be bound in heaven, and whatever you loose on earth shall be loosed in heaven. Matthew 16:19

Truly, I say to you, whatever you bind on earth shall be bound in heaven, and whatever you loose on earth shall be loosed in heaven. Again I say to you, if two of you agree on earth about anything they ask, it will be done for them by my Father in heaven. For where two or three are gathered in my name, there am I among them." Matthew 18:18-20

If you forgive the sins of any, they are forgiven them; if you withhold forgiveness from any, it is withheld. John 20:23

Blessings (God's)

"And if you faithfully obey the voice of the Lord your God, being careful to do all his commandments that I command you today, the Lord your God will set you high above all the nations of the earth. 2 And all these blessings shall come upon you and overtake you, if you obey the voice of the Lord your God. 3 Blessed shall you be in the city, and blessed shall you be in the field. 4 Blessed shall be the fruit of your womb and the fruit of your ground and the fruit of your cattle, the increase of your herds and the young of your flock. 5 Blessed shall be your basket and your kneading bowl. 6 Blessed shall you be when you come in, and blessed shall you be when you go out. Deuteronomy 28:1-6

Oh, taste and see that the Lord is good! Blessed is the man who takes refuge in him! Psalm 34:8

The blessing of the Lord makes rich, and he adds no sorrow with it. Proverbs 10:22

When a man's ways please the Lord, he makes even his enemies to be at peace with him. Proverbs 16:7

If you are willing and obedient, you shall eat the good of the land; Isaiah 1:19

"Blessed is the man who trusts in the Lord, whose trust is the Lord. He is like a tree planted by water, that sends out its roots by the stream, and does not fear when heat comes, for its leaves remain green, and is not anxious in the year of drought, for it does not cease to bear fruit." Jeremiah 17:7-8

Everyone also to whom God has given wealth and possessions and power to enjoy them, and to accept his lot and rejoice in his toil—this is the gift of God. Ecclesiastes 5:19

"Blessed are those who hunger and thirst for righteousness, for they shall be satisfied." Matthew 5:6

Give, and it will be given to you. Good measure, pressed down, shaken together, running over, will be put into your lap. For with the measure you use it will be measured back to you. Luke 6:38

But, as it is written, "What no eye has seen, nor ear heard, nor the heart of man imagined, what God has prepared for those who love him"— 1 Corinthians 2:9

And God is able to make all grace abound to you, so that having all sufficiency in all things at all times, you may abound in every good work. As it is written, "He has distributed freely, he has given to the poor; his righteousness endures forever." He who supplies seed to the sower and bread for food will supply and multiply your seed for sowing and increase the harvest of your righteousness. 2 Corinthians 9:8-10

Blessed be the God and Father of our Lord Jesus Christ, who has blessed us in Christ with every spiritual blessing in the heavenly places, Ephesians 1:3

Blessed is the man who remains steadfast under trial, for when he has stood the test he will receive the crown of life, which God has promised to those who love him. James 1:12

Every good gift and every perfect gift is from above, coming down from the Father of lights with whom there is no variation or shadow due to change. James 1:17

The Blood of Jesus

The blood shall be a sign for you, on the houses where you are. And when I see the blood, I will pass over you, and no plague will befall you to destroy you, when I strike the land of Egypt. Exodus 12:13

For this is my blood of the covenant, which is poured out for many for the forgiveness of sins. Matthew 26:28

Pay careful attention to yourselves and to all the flock, in which the Holy Spirit has made you overseers, to care for the church of God, which he obtained with his own blood. Acts 20:28

Whom God put forward as a propitiation by his blood, to be received by faith. This was to show God's righteousness, because in his divine forbearance he had passed over former sins. Romans 3:25

In him we have redemption through his blood, the forgiveness of our trespasses, according to the riches of his grace . . . Ephesians 1:7

But now in Christ Jesus you who once were far off have been brought near by the blood of Christ. Ephesians 2:13

How much more will the blood of Christ, who through the eternal Spirit offered himself without blemish to God, purify our conscience from dead works to serve the living God. Hebrews 9:14

Indeed, under the law almost everything is purified with blood, and without the shedding of blood there is no forgiveness of sins. Hebrews 9:22

According to the foreknowledge of God the Father, in the sanctification of the Spirit, for obedience to Jesus Christ and for sprinkling with his blood: May grace and peace be multiplied to you. 1 Peter 1:2

Knowing that you were ransomed from the futile ways inherited from your forefathers, not with perishable things such as silver or gold, but with the precious blood of Christ, like that of a lamb without blemish or spot. 1 Peter 1:18-19

But if we walk in the light, as he is in the light, we have fellowship with one another, and the blood of Jesus his Son cleanses us from all sin. If we say we have no sin, we deceive ourselves, and the truth is not in us. If we confess our sins, he is faithful and just to forgive us our sins and to cleanse us from all unrighteousness. 1 John 1:7-9

Boldness

Be strong and courageous. Do not fear or be in dread of them, for it is the Lord your God who goes with you. He will not leave you or forsake you. Deuteronomy 31:6

Then David said to Solomon his son, "Be strong and courageous and do it. Do not be afraid and do not be dismayed, for the Lord God, even my God, is with you. He will not leave you or forsake you, until all the work for the service of the house of the Lord is finished." 1 Chronicles 28:20

Of David. The Lord is my light and my salvation; whom shall I fear? The Lord is the stronghold of my life; of whom shall I be afraid?
Psalm 27:1

Have I not commanded you? Be strong and courageous. Do not be frightened, and do not be dismayed, for the Lord your God is with you wherever you go. Joshua 1:9

Let us then with confidence draw near to the throne of grace, that we may receive mercy and find grace to help in time of need. Hebrews 4:16

As it is my eager expectation and hope that I will not be at all ashamed, but that with full courage now as always Christ will be honored in my body, whether by life or by death. Philippians 1:20

Keep your life free from love of money, and be content with what you have, for he has said, "I will never leave you nor forsake you." So we can confidently say, "The Lord is my helper; I will not fear; what can man do to me?" Hebrews 13:5-6

Praying at all times in the Spirit, with all prayer and supplication. To that end keep alert with all perseverance, making supplication for all the saints, and also for me, that words may be given to me in opening my mouth boldly to proclaim the mystery of the gospel, for which I am an ambassador in chains, that I may declare it boldly, as I ought to speak. Ephesians 6:18-20

The wicked flee when no one pursues, but the righteous are bold as a lion. Proverbs 28:1

Business – Work/Job Related

You shall remember the Lord your God, for it is he who gives you power to get wealth, that he may confirm his covenant that he swore to your fathers, as it is this day. Deuteronomy 8:18

It is well with the man who deals generously and lends; who conducts his affairs with justice. Psalm 112:5

A slack hand causes poverty, but the hand of the diligent makes rich. Proverbs 10:4

Wealth gained hastily will dwindle, but whoever gathers little by little will increase it. Proverbs 13:11

Commit your work to the Lord, and your plans will be established. Proverbs 16:3

Better is a little with righteousness than great revenues with injustice. Proverbs 16:8

Whoever oppresses the poor to increase his own wealth, or gives to the rich, will only come to poverty. Proverbs 22:16

Do you see a man skillful in his work? He will stand before kings; he will not stand before obscure men. Proverbs 22:29

No one can serve two masters, for either he will hate the one and love the other, or he will be devoted to the one and despise the other. You cannot serve God and money. Matthew 6:24

Pay to all what is owed to them: taxes to whom taxes are owed, revenue to whom revenue is owed, respect to whom respect is owed, honor to whom honor is owed. Romans 13:7

And whatever you do, in Word or deed, do everything in the name of the Lord Jesus, giving thanks to God the Father through him. Colossians 3:17

Whatever you do, work heartily, as for the Lord and not for men. Colossians 3:23

For the Scripture says, "You shall not muzzle an ox when it treads out the grain," and, "The laborer deserves his wages." 1 Timothy 5:18

Child Rearing

"Honor your father and your mother, that your days may be long in the land that the Lord your God is giving you." Exodus 20:12

Even if my father and mother should desert me, you will take care of me. Psalm 27:10 CEV

Behold, children are a heritage from the Lord, the fruit of the womb a reward. Like arrows in the hand of a warrior are the children of one's youth. Blessed is the man who fills his quiver with them! He shall not be put to shame when he speaks with his enemies in the gate. Psalm 127:3-5

Hear, my son, your father's instruction, and forsake not your mother's teaching, for they are a graceful garland for your head and pendants for your neck. Proverbs 1:8-9

My son, do not despise the Lord's discipline or be weary of his reproof, for the Lord reproves him whom he loves, as a father the son in whom he delights. Proverbs 3:11-12

A good man leaves an inheritance to his children's children, but the sinner's wealth is laid up for the righteous. Proverbs 13:22

Whoever spares the rod hates his son, but he who loves him is diligent to discipline him. Proverbs 13:24

Even a child makes himself known by his acts, by whether his conduct is pure and upright. Proverbs 20:11

Train up a child in the way he should go; even when he is old he will not depart from it. Proverbs 22:6

Folly is bound up in the heart of a child, but the rod of discipline drives it far from him. Proverbs 22:15

The rod and reproof give wisdom, but a child left to himself brings shame to his mother. Proverbs 29:15

Fathers, do not provoke your children to anger, but bring them up in the discipline and instruction of the Lord. Ephesians 6:4

Fathers, do not provoke your children, lest they become discouraged. Colossians 3:21

And have you forgotten the exhortation that addresses you as sons? "My son, do not regard lightly the discipline of the Lord, nor be weary when reproved by him. For the Lord disciplines the one he loves, and chastises every son whom he receives." It is for discipline that you have to endure. God is treating you as sons. For what son is there whom his father does not discipline? If you are left without discipline, in which all have participated, then you are illegitimate children and not sons. Besides this, we have had earthly fathers who disciplined us and we respected them. Shall we not much more be subject to the Father of spirits and live? Hebrews 12:5-9

Children's Daily Affirmation for Divine Wholeness

As a child of the Most High God – Elohim – I am called to walk in love and obedience to God's will.

Therefore, I speak and declare that:

I AM LOVE. I AM KINDNESS. I AM OBEDIENCE. I AM RESPECTFUL. I AM BEAUTIFUL. I AM SMART, AND I always make wise choices.

When I am at home, at school, or anywhere: I will do as I am told by those who are responsible for me; the FIRST time.

I complete all of my work and chores, the first time. I AM a leader and a good example. I pay attention and follow instructions. I speak with wisdom – knowing when to ask for help and stand in truth. I behave with honor, making God, my teachers, my family, and myself proud.

I can do ALL things with the help of Jesus Christ. I AM also a WINNER who Loves God and is called for His purpose – so ALL things are working for my good.

I was created by God in His image – therefore, I am Royalty! My worth, beauty, and value came from God when He created me, and will always be. God loves me; therefore, I love others as I love and respect myself and Christ inside me. I have been blessed with gifts, talents, and abilities to serve God's Divine purpose for my life on this earth. And I will complete my assignment — for His Glory, my good, and the good of others. And it is so!

Comfort

You will increase my greatness and comfort me again. Psalm 71:21

Even though I walk through the valley of the shadow of death, I will fear no evil, for you are with me; your rod and your staff, they comfort me. Psalm 23:4

For his anger is but for a moment, and his favor is for a lifetime. Weeping may tarry for the night, but joy comes with the morning. Psalm 30:5

The Lord is near to the brokenhearted and saves the crushed in spirit. Psalm 34:18

He who dwells in the shelter of the Most High will abide in the shadow of the Almighty. I will say to the Lord, "My refuge and my fortress, my God, in whom I trust." For he will deliver you from the snare of the fowler and from the deadly pestilence. He will cover you with his pinions, and under his wings, you will find refuge; his faithfulness is a shield and buckler. You will not fear the terror of the night nor the arrow that flies by day . . . Psalm 91:1-5

I love the Lord because he has heard my voice and my pleas for mercy. Because he inclined his ear to me; therefore, I will call on him as long as I live. Psalm 116:1-2

He gives power to the faint, and to him who has no might, he increases strength. Even youths shall faint and be weary, and young men shall fall exhausted, but they who wait for the Lord shall renew their strength; they shall mount up with wings like eagles; they shall run and not be weary; they shall walk and not faint. Isaiah 40:29-31

Seeing the crowds, he went up on the mountain, and when he sat down, his disciples came to him. And he opened his mouth and taught them, saying: "Blessed are the poor in spirit, for theirs is the kingdom of heaven. "Blessed are those who mourn, for they shall be comforted. "Blessed are the meek, for they shall inherit the earth. Matthew 5:1-5

Come to me, all who labor and are heavy laden, and I will give you rest. Take my yoke upon you, and learn from me, for I am gentle and lowly in heart, and you will find rest for your souls. For my yoke is easy, and my burden is light. Matthew 11:28-30

May the God of hope fill you with all joy and peace in believing, so that by the power of the Holy Spirit you may abound in hope. Romans 15:13

Blessed be the God and Father of our Lord Jesus Christ, the Father of mercies and God of all comfort, who comforts us in all our affliction, so that we may be able to comfort those who are in any affliction, with the comfort with which we ourselves are comforted by God.
2 Corinthians 1:3-4

Condemnation (Guilt)

Whoever believes in him is not condemned, but whoever does not believe is condemned already, because he has not believed in the name of the only Son of God. John 3:18

Therefore, since we have been justified by faith, we have peace with God through our Lord Jesus Christ. Romans 5:1

There is therefore now no condemnation for those who are in Christ Jesus. For the law of the Spirit of life has set you free in Christ Jesus from the law of sin and death. For God has done what the law, weakened by the flesh, could not do. By sending his own Son in the likeness of

37

sinful flesh and for sin, he condemned sin in the flesh, in order that the righteous requirement of the law might be fulfilled in us, who walk not according to the flesh but according to the Spirit. For those who live according to the flesh set their minds on the things of the flesh, but those who live according to the Spirit set their minds on the things of the Spirit. Romans 8:1-5

You foolish Galatians, who has bewitched you, before whose eyes Jesus Christ was publicly portrayed as crucified? 2 This is the only thing I want to find out from you: did you receive the Spirit by the works of the Law, or by hearing with faith? 3 Are you so foolish? Having begun by the Spirit, are you now being perfected by the flesh? 4 Did you [suffer so many things in vain—if indeed it was in vain? 5 So then, does He who provides you with the Spirit and works miracles among you, do it by the works of the Law, or by hearing with faith. Galatians 3:1-5 NASB

For as many as are of the works of the Law are under a curse; for it is written, "Cursed is everyone who does not abide by all things written in the book of the law, to perform them." Galatians 3:10 NASB

Confession (Sin – Faith)

I acknowledged my sin to you, and I did not cover my iniquity; I said, "I will confess my transgressions to the Lord," and you forgave the iniquity of my sin. Selah. Psalm 32:5

Whoever conceals his transgressions will not prosper, but he who confesses and forsakes them will obtain mercy. Proverbs 28:13

The times of ignorance God overlooked, but now he commands all people everywhere to repent . . . Acts 17:30

Because, if you confess with your mouth that Jesus is Lord and believe in your heart that God raised him from the dead, you will be saved. Romans 10:9

Through him then let us continually offer up a sacrifice of praise to God, that is, the fruit of lips that acknowledge his name. Hebrews 13:15

So whoever knows the right thing to do and fails to do it, for him it is sin. James 4:17

Therefore, confess your sins to one another and pray for one another, that you may be healed. The prayer of a righteous person has great power as it is working. James 5:16

If we confess our sins, he is faithful and just to forgive us our sins and to cleanse us from all unrighteousness. 1 John 1:9

Whoever confesses that Jesus is the Son of God, God abides in him, and he in God. 1 John 4:15

Confidence

Have I not commanded you? Be strong and courageous. Do not be frightened, and do not be dismayed, for the Lord your God is with you wherever you go. Joshua 1:9

The Lord will fulfill his purpose for me; your steadfast love, O Lord, endures forever. Do not forsake the work of your hands. Psalm 138:8

In all your ways acknowledge him, and he will make straight your paths. Proverbs 3:6

For the Lord will be your confidence and will keep your foot from being caught. Proverbs 3:26

Truly, truly, I say to you, whoever hears my Word and believes him who sent me has eternal life. He does not come into judgment, but has passed from death to life. John 5:24

For I am sure that neither death nor life, nor angels nor rulers, nor things present nor things to come, nor powers, nor height nor depth, nor anything else in all creation, will be able to separate us from the love of God in Christ Jesus our Lord. Romans 8:38-39

And I was with you in weakness and in fear and much trembling, and my speech and my message were not in plausible words of wisdom, but in demonstration of the Spirit and of power, that your faith might not rest in the wisdom of men but in the power of God. 1 Corinthians 2:3-5

I can do all things through him who strengthens me. Philippians 4:13

Let us then with confidence draw near to the throne of grace, that we may receive mercy and find grace to help in time of need. Hebrews 4:16

Therefore do not throw away your confidence, which has a great reward. For you have need of endurance, so that when you have done the will of God you may receive what is promised. Hebrews 10:35-36

So we can confidently say, "The Lord is my helper; I will not fear; what can man do to me?" Hebrews 13:6

Let no one despise you for your youth, but set the believers an example in speech, in conduct, in love, in faith, in purity. 1 Timothy 4:12

Confusion

All of them are put to shame and confounded; the makers of idols go in confusion together. Isaiah 45:16

But the Helper, the Holy Spirit, whom the Father will send in my name, he will teach you all things and bring to your remembrance all that I have said to you. John 14:26

When the Spirit of truth comes, he will guide you into all the truth, for he will not speak on his own authority, but whatever he hears he will speak, and he will declare to you the things that are to come. John 16:13

For the law of the Spirit of life has set you free in Christ Jesus from the law of sin and death. Romans 8:2

For God is not a God of confusion but of peace. As in all the churches of the saints . . . 1 Corinthians 14:33

Therefore, if anyone is in Christ, he is a new creation. The old has passed away; behold, the new has come. 2 Corinthians 5:17

But even if we or an angel from heaven should preach to you a gospel contrary to the one we preached to you, let him be accursed. As we have said before, so now I say again: If anyone is preaching to you a gospel contrary to the one you received, let him be accursed. Galatians 1:8-9

Think over what I say, for the Lord will give you understanding in everything. 2 Timothy 2:7

Keep your life free from love of money, and be content with what you have, for he has said, "I will never leave you nor forsake you." Hebrews 13:5

Beloved, do not believe every spirit, but test the spirits to see whether they are from God, for many false prophets have gone out into the world. 1 John 4:1

Contentment (Joy – Happiness)

Better is a little with righteousness than great revenues with injustice. Proverbs 16:8

Better is a poor man who walks in his integrity than a rich man who is crooked in his ways. Proverbs 28:6

Remove far from me falsehood and lying; give me neither poverty nor riches; feed me with the food that is needful for me, lest I be full and deny you and say, "Who is the Lord?" or lest I be poor and steal and profane the name of my God. Proverbs 30:8-9

"Therefore I tell you, do not be anxious about your life, what you will eat or what you will drink, nor about your body, what you will put on. Is not life more than food, and the body more than clothing?" Matthew 6:25

And why are you worried about clothing? Observe how the lilies of the field grow; they do not toil nor do they spin, 29 yet I say to you that not even Solomon in all his glory clothed himself like one of these. 30 But if God so clothes the grass of the field, which is alive today and tomorrow is thrown into the furnace, will He not much more clothe you? You of little faith! 31 Do not worry then, saying, 'What will we eat?' or 'What will we drink?' or 'What will we wear for clothing?' 32 For the Gentiles eagerly seek all these things; for your heavenly Father knows that you need all these things. 33 But seek first His kingdom and His righteousness, and all these things will be added to you. 34 "So do not worry about tomorrow; for tomorrow will care for itself. Each day has enough trouble of its own. Matthew 6:28-34 NASB

Soldiers also asked him, "And we, what shall we do?" And he said to them, "Do not extort money from anyone by threats or by false accusation, and be content with your wages." Luke 3:14

And he said to them, "Take care, and be on your guard against all covetousness, for one's life does not consist in the abundance of his possessions." Luke 12:15

Not that I am speaking of being in need, for I have learned in whatever situation I am to be content. I know how to be brought low, and I know how to abound. In any and every circumstance, I have learned the secret of facing plenty and hunger, abundance and need. I can do all things through him who strengthens me. Philippians 4:11-13

Only let each person lead the life that the Lord has assigned to him, and to which God has called him. This is my rule in all the churches.
1 Corinthians 7:17

For the sake of Christ, then, I am content with weaknesses, insults, hardships, persecutions, and calamities. For when I am weak, then I am strong. 2 Corinthians 12:10

But godliness with contentment is great gain, for we brought nothing into the world, and we cannot take anything out of the world. But if we have food and clothing, with these we will be content. But those who desire to be rich fall into temptation, into a snare, into many senseless and harmful desires that plunge people into ruin and destruction.1 Timothy 6:6-9

For the love of money is a root of all kinds of evils. It is through this craving that some have wandered away from the faith and pierced themselves with many pangs. But as for you, O man of God, flee these things. Pursue righteousness, godliness, faith, love, steadfastness, gentleness. 1 Timothy 6:10-11

Humble yourselves, therefore, under the mighty hand of God so that at the proper time he may exalt you, casting all your anxieties on him, because he cares for you. 1 Peter 5:6-7

Counsel (Wise Vs. Unwise)

How blessed is the man who does not walk in the counsel of the wicked, Nor stand in the path of sinners, Nor sit in the seat of scoffers! 2 But his delight is in the law of the Lord, And in His law he meditates day and night.3 He will be like a tree firmly planted by streams of water, Which yields its fruit in its season And its leaf does not wither; And in whatever he does, he prospers. 4 The wicked are not so, But they are like chaff which the wind drives away. 5 Therefore the wicked will not stand in the judgment, Nor sinners in the assembly of the righteous. 6 For the Lord knows the way of the righteous, But the way of the wicked will perish. Psalm 1:1-6 NASB

I will instruct you and teach you in the way you should go; I will counsel you with my eye upon you. Psalm 32:8

The Lord brings the counsel of the nations to nothing; he frustrates the plans of the peoples. The counsel of the Lord stands forever, the plans of his heart to all generations. Blessed is the nation whose God is the Lord, the people whom he has chosen as his heritage! The Lord looks down from heaven; he sees all the children of man; from where he sits enthroned he looks out on all the inhabitants of the earth, . . .
Psalm 33:10-14

The fear of the Lord is the beginning of knowledge; fools despise wisdom and instruction. Proverbs 1:7

My son, do not forget my teaching, but let your heart keep my commandments, for length of days and years of life and peace they will add to you. Let not steadfast love and faithfulness forsake you; bind them around your neck; write them on the tablet of your heart. So you will find favor and good success in the sight of God and man. Proverbs 3:1-4

Where there is no guidance, a people falls, but in an abundance of counselors there is safety. Proverbs 11:14

The way of a fool is right in his own eyes, but a wise man listens to advice. Proverbs 12:15

Listen to advice and accept instruction, that you may gain wisdom in the future. Many are the plans in the mind of a man, but it is the purpose of the Lord that will stand. Proverbs 19:20-21

Better was a poor and wise youth than an old and foolish king who no longer knew how to take advice. Ecclesiastes 4:13

Do not be deceived: "Bad company ruins good morals."
1 Corinthians 15:33

All Scripture is breathed out by God and profitable for teaching, for reproof, for correction, and for training in righteousness,
2 Timothy 3:16

If any of you lacks wisdom, let him ask God, who gives generously to all without reproach, and it will be given him. James 1:5

But the wisdom from above is first pure, then peaceable, gentle, open to reason, full of mercy and good fruits, impartial and sincere. And a harvest of righteousness is sown in peace by those who make peace. James 3:17-18

Death

Even though I walk through the valley of the shadow of death, I will fear no evil, for you are with me; your rod and your staff, they comfort me. Psalm 23:4

Precious in the sight of the Lord is the death of his saints. Psalm 116:15

Jesus said to her, "I am the resurrection and the life. Whoever believes in me, though he die, yet shall he live, and everyone who lives and believes in me shall never die. Do you believe this?" John 11:25-26

Do not let your heart be troubled; believe in God, believe also in Me. 2 In My Father's house are many dwelling places; if it were not so, I would have told you; for I go to prepare a place for you. 3 If I go and prepare a place for you, I will come again and receive you to Myself, that where I am, there you may be also. John 14:1-3 NASB

For if we live, we live to the Lord, and if we die, we die to the Lord. So then, whether we live or whether we die, we are the Lord's. Romans 14:8

So also is the resurrection of the dead. It is sown a perishable body, it is raised an imperishable body; 43 it is sown in dishonor, it is raised in glory; it is sown in weakness, it is raised in power; 44 it is sown a natural body, it is raised a spiritual body. If there is a natural body, there is also a spiritual body. 1 Corinthians 15:42-44 NASB

Behold, I tell you a mystery; we will not all sleep, but we will all be changed, 52 in a moment, in the twinkling of an eye, at the last trumpet; for the trumpet will sound, and the dead will be raised imperishable, and we will be changed. 53 For this perishable must put on the imperishable, and this mortal must put on immortality. 54 But when this perishable will have put on the imperishable, and this mortal will have put on immortality, then will come about the saying that is written, "Death is swallowed up in victory. 55 O death, where is your victory? O death, where is your sting?" 56 The sting of death is sin, and the power of sin is the law; 57 but thanks be to God, who gives us the victory through our Lord Jesus Christ. 1 Corinthians 15:51-57 NASB

But we do not want you to be uninformed, brethren, about those who are asleep, so that you will not grieve as do the rest who have no hope. 14 For if we believe that Jesus died and rose again, even so God will bring with Him those who have fallen asleep in Jesus. 15 For this we say to you by the word of the Lord, that we who are alive and remain until the coming of the Lord, will not precede those who have fallen asleep. 16 For the Lord Himself will descend from heaven with a shout, with the voice of the archangel and with the trumpet of God, and the dead in Christ will rise first. 17 Then we who are alive and remain will be caught up together with them in the clouds to meet the Lord in the air, and so we shall always be with the Lord. 18 Therefore comfort one another with these words. 1 Thessalonians 4:13-18 NASB

And I heard a voice from heaven, saying, "Write, 'Blessed are the dead who die in the Lord from now on!'" "Yes," says the Spirit, "so that they may rest from their labors, for their deeds follow with them." Revelation 14:13 NASB

"He will wipe away every tear from their eyes, and death shall be no more, neither shall there be mourning, nor crying, nor pain anymore, for the former things have passed away." Revelation 21:4

Debt – Credit/Money Problems

For the Lord your God will bless you, as he promised you, and you shall lend to many nations, but you shall not borrow, and you shall rule over many nations, but they shall not rule over you. Deuteronomy 15:6

At the end of every seven years you shall grant a remission of debts. 2 This is the manner of remission: every creditor shall release what he has loaned to his neighbor; he shall not exact it of his neighbor and his brother, because the Lord's remission has been proclaimed. 3 From a foreigner you may exact it, but your hand shall release whatever of yours is with your brother. 4 However, there will be no poor among you, since the Lord will surely bless you in the land which the Lord your God is giving you as an inheritance to possess, 5 if only you listen obediently to the voice of the Lord your God, to observe carefully all this commandment which I am commanding you today. 6 For the Lord your God will bless you as He has promised you, and you will lend to many nations, but you will not borrow; and you will rule over many nations, but they will not rule over you. Deuteronomy 15:1-6 NASB

The wicked borrows but does not pay back, but the righteous is generous and gives; Psalm 37:21

Honor the Lord with your wealth and with the firstfruits of all your produce; Proverbs 3:9

Wealth gained hastily will dwindle, but whoever gathers little by little will increase it. Proverbs 13:11

The rich rules over the poor, and the borrower is the slave of the lender. Proverbs 22:7

It is better that you should not vow than that you should vow and not pay. Ecclesiastes 5:5

He who loves money will not be satisfied with money, nor he who loves wealth with his income; this also is vanity. Ecclesiastes 5:10

And if you lend to those from whom you expect to receive, what credit is that to you? Even sinners lend to sinners, to get back the same amount. But love your enemies, and do good, and lend, expecting nothing in return, and your reward will be great, and you will be sons of the Most High, for he is kind to the ungrateful and the evil. Luke 6:34-35

For which of you, desiring to build a tower, does not first sit down and count the cost, whether he has enough to complete it? Luke 14:28

"One who is faithful in a very little is also faithful in much, and one who is dishonest in a very little is also dishonest in much." Luke 16:10

Pay to all what is owed to them: taxes to whom taxes are owed, revenue to whom revenue is owed, respect to whom respect is owed, honor to whom honor is owed. Owe no one anything, except to love each other, for the one who loves another has fulfilled the law. Romans 13:7-8

And my God will supply every need of yours according to his riches in glory in Christ Jesus. Philippians 4:19

But if anyone does not provide for his relatives, and especially for members of his household, he has denied the faith and is worse than an unbeliever. 1 Timothy 5:8

For the love of money is a root of all kinds of evils. It is through this craving that some have wandered away from the faith and pierced themselves with many pangs. 1 Timothy 6:10

Keep your life free from love of money, and be content with what you have, for he has said, "I will never leave you nor forsake you." Hebrews 13:5

Depression–Heartache

When the righteous cry for help, the Lord hears and delivers them out of all their troubles. The Lord is near to the brokenhearted and saves the crushed in spirit. Psalm 34:17-18

To the choirmaster. A Psalm of David. I waited patiently for the Lord; he inclined to me and heard my cry. He drew me up from the pit of destruction, out of the miry bog, and set my feet upon a rock, making my steps secure. He put a new song in my mouth, a song of praise to our God. Many will see and fear, and put their trust in the Lord.
Psalm 40:1-3

Why are you cast down, O my soul, and why are you in turmoil within me? Hope in God; for I shall again praise him, my salvation. Psalm 42:5

When the cares of my heart are many, your consolations cheer my soul. Psalm 94:19

Answer me quickly, O Lord! My spirit fails! Hide not your face from me, lest I be like those who go down to the pit. Let me hear in the morning of your steadfast love, for in you I trust. Make me know the way I should go, for to you I lift up my soul. Psalm 143:7-8

Anxiety in a man's heart weighs him down, but a good word makes him glad. Proverbs 12:25

But they who wait for the Lord shall renew their strength; they shall mount up with wings like eagles; they shall run and not be weary; they shall walk and not faint. Isaiah 40:31

Fear not, for I am with you; be not dismayed, for I am your God; I will strengthen you, I will help you, I will uphold you with my righteous right hand. Isaiah 41:10

May the God of hope fill you with all joy and peace in believing, so that by the power of the Holy Spirit you may abound in hope. Romans 15:13

Finally, brothers, whatever is true, whatever is honorable, whatever is just, whatever is pure, whatever is lovely, whatever is commendable, if there is any excellence, if there is anything worthy of praise, think about these things. Philippians 4:8

Humble yourselves, therefore, under the mighty hand of God so that at the proper time he may exalt you, casting all your anxieties on him, because he cares for you. 1 Peter 5:6-7

Deliverance

If my people who are called by my name humble themselves, and pray and seek my face and turn from their wicked ways, then I will hear from heaven and will forgive their sin and heal their land. 2 Chronicles 7:14

You will not need to fight in this battle. Stand firm, hold your position, and see the salvation of the Lord on your behalf, O Judah and Jerusalem. Do not be afraid and do not be dismayed. Tomorrow go out against them, and the Lord will be with you. 2 Chronicles 20:17

I sought the Lord, and he answered me and delivered me from all my fears. Psalm 34:4

When the righteous cry for help, the Lord hears and delivers them out of all their troubles. Psalm 34:17

As for me, I am poor and needy, but the Lord takes thought for me. You are my help and my deliverer; do not delay, O my God! Psalm 40:17

"And call upon me in the day of trouble; I will deliver you, and you shall glorify me." Psalm 50:15

He who dwells in the shelter of the Most High will abide in the shadow of the Almighty. 2 I will say to the Lord, "My refuge and my fortress, My God, in whom I trust!" 3 For it is He who delivers you from the snare of the trapper And from the deadly pestilence. 4 He will cover you with His pinions, And under His wings you may seek refuge; His faithfulness is a shield and bulwark. 5 You will not be afraid of the terror by night, Or of the arrow that flies by day; Psalm 91:1-5 NASB

Then they cried to the Lord in their trouble, and he delivered them from their distress. Psalm 107:6

Remember not the former things, nor consider the things of old. Behold, I am doing a new thing; now it springs forth, do you not perceive it? I will make a way in the wilderness and rivers in the desert. Isaiah 43:18-19

"No weapon that is formed against you will prosper; And every tongue that accuses you in judgment you will condemn. This is the heritage of the servants of the Lord, And their vindication is from Me," declares the Lord. Isaiah 54:17

"And you will know the truth, and the truth will set you free." John 8:32

No temptation has overtaken you that is not common to man. God is faithful, and he will not let you be tempted beyond your ability, but with the temptation he will also provide the way of escape, that you may be able to endure it. 1 Corinthians 10:13

But the Lord is faithful. He will establish you and guard you against the evil one. 2 Thessalonians 3:3

For freedom Christ has set us free; stand firm therefore, and do not submit again to a yoke of slavery. Galatians 5:1

Submit yourselves therefore to God. Resist the devil, and he will flee from you. James 4:7

The Lord will rescue me from every evil deed and bring me safely into his heavenly kingdom. To him be the glory forever and ever. Amen. 2 Timothy 4:18

Then the Lord knows how to rescue the godly from trials, and to keep the unrighteous under punishment until the day of judgment- 2 Peter 2:9

Affirmations for Total Freedom of the Divine Self

The power of God is working through me, to free me of every negative influence. All power is given unto me for good in my mind, body, and affairs, and I rightly use it now!

I let go of everything not Divinely designed for me, and the perfect plan of my life now comes to pass.

The light of Christ within me now wipes out all fear, doubt, anger, and resentment. God's love pours through me, an irresistible magnetic current. I see only perfection and draw to me my own.

I now smash and demolish by my spoken word, every untrue record of my subconscious mind. They shall return to the dust-heap of their native nothingness, for they came from my own vain imaginings. I now make my NEW perfect records through the Christ within me; the records of health, wealth, love, and perfect self-expression.

Prayer for Deliverance
Addiction (Alcohol, Drugs, Sex)
(Modified from ibelieve.com)

God, my Father, help me to turn my eyes toward you. My help comes from You, who made all things (Psalm 121). You alone possess the power to break the chains of my addiction and break down the bars of this prison. Release me from the bondage of **(addiction name)**. Return me to my family and true friends. Restore what has been stolen. I do not possess the strength, but through Jesus, I can do anything (Philippians 4:13). Give me the strength to say no and turn my eyes to You.

Father, wipe away the fog in my mind and let me see clearly the deception of the enemy, who comes only to kill and destroy. Open my eyes to see the lies. Give me the vision to see who I am in You. How do you see me? Help me to know your love. Let nothing but a clear vision of who I am to You and the knowledge of your love satisfy every desire.

God, I need your help. I cannot stop this desire on my own. I receive your promise to always be near. You are my strength; come quickly to help me (Psalm 22:19). I receive Your promise to forgive my sins through Jesus, and humbly ask that You forgive me for the things I have done, said, and thought under the spell of addiction. Forgive me for straying from Your way and going my own way. Father, pull me from this pit and order my steps on the path that leads to you (Psalm 40:1).

Thank you, Father, for protecting me from mortal harm. Thank you for the grace that brought me to this place, seeking you. Thank you for the healing to come. Thank you that you are a Father of second chances, giving grace when it is needed most. I receive Your deliverance NOW! I believe that I am free, I walk in grace and righteousness through the Power of Jesus Christ within me, and receive Your promise, that whom the Son sets free, is free indeed (John 8:36)! In Jesus' name, by the power of Your Divine Spirit.

Prayer for Deliverance
Soul-Ties/ Ungodly Attachments
(Modified from missionariesofprayer.org)

"Father God, I thank you for saving me from destruction. I praise you for sending Jesus to die for my sins. Please, forgive me for my sins against you. Specifically, I confess that I _____ (details of the sin & names). I repent of that sin and renounce it now. Lord, please purify my heart from this sin, the memory of it, and any associated fantasy I have entertained in my mind regarding it.

In the name of Jesus Christ and by the power of his blood, shed on the cross, I cut myself free from any soul ties that may have been established with _____ (name(s) or specific objects). I commit him/her/them to the care of Jesus Christ for Him to do with as He wills. Satan, the Lord rebuke you in all your works and ways. May the power of Christ rebuke any evil spirits that have a foothold in me. In the name of Jesus, I command you evil spirits to leave me and go directly to Jesus Christ. Father, please heal my soul of any wounds resulting from these soul ties. Please reintegrate any part of me that may have been detained through this/these soul ties and restore me to wholeness. I also ask that you reintegrate any part of the person(s) I sinned with that have been detained in me, and restore them to wholeness. Thank you, Lord, for your healing power and your perfect love for me. May I glorify you with my life from this point forward. In Jesus' name, Amen."

Discouragement

It is the Lord who goes before you. He will be with you; he will not leave you or forsake you. Do not fear or be dismayed. Deuteronomy 31:8

Have I not commanded you? Be strong and courageous. Do not be frightened, and do not be dismayed, for the Lord your God is with you wherever you go. Joshua 1:9

I have said these things to you, that in me you may have peace. In the world you will have tribulation. But take heart; I have overcome the world. John 16:33

Therefore, my beloved brothers, be steadfast, immovable, always abounding in the work of the Lord, knowing that in the Lord your labor is not in vain. 1 Corinthians 15:58

But he said to me, "My grace is sufficient for you, for my power is made perfect in weakness." Therefore I will boast all the more gladly of my weaknesses, so that the power of Christ may rest upon me.
2 Corinthians 12:9

For this light momentary affliction is preparing for us an eternal weight of glory beyond all comparison, as we look not to the things that are seen but to the things that are unseen. For the things that are seen are transient, but the things that are unseen are eternal. 2 Corinthians 4:17-18

What then shall we say to these things? If God is for us, who can be against us? Romans 8:31

Therefore, since we are surrounded by so great a cloud of witnesses, let us also lay aside every weight, and sin which clings so closely, and let us run with endurance the race that is set before us . . . Hebrews 12:1

Reflections on Divorce

And Pharisees came up and in order to test him asked, "Is it lawful for a man to divorce his wife?" He answered them, "What did Moses command you?" They said, "Moses allowed a man to write a certificate of divorce and to send her away." And Jesus said to them, "Because of your hardness of heart he wrote you this commandment. But from the beginning of creation, 'God made them male and female.' Mark 10:2-12

My idea for this book came after years of using 'the Scripture Keys for Kingdom Living' by June Davis to reference, learn, and memorize scripture. However, I always had an issue with the King's English and truly got tripped up on words like "thus," "thither," and the like. Although I still use it to this day, I also took issue with some of the scripture references, either not relating to modern-day life or being presented in an archaic light. Furthermore, I continue to give them out as gifts because I believe the positives outweigh the negatives.

That said, one of my main issues was how the topic of divorce was presented. Of course, all the scriptures about divorced people who did so for reasons other than sexual immorality or adultery were listed. However, I refuse to believe that repentant murderers, liars, abusers, and so on can be TOTALLY forgiven by God, while people who enter marriage ill-advisedly, or unaware of how to love someone unconditionally or are broken, bruised, and totally incapable of loving themselves let alone anyone else, are considered to be living in perpetual sin if they divorce for reasons other than sexual immorality.

Therefore, I rest on Mark 10:2-12, where Jesus is tested by the Pharisees on the topic of divorce, and His answers as to why it was granted. In a nutshell, He says that it was granted due to that "hardness of hearts," which simply means an unwillingness to bend, give in, or soften to change by either one or both individuals. The truth of the matter is that God can heal anything and anyone. Nothing is too hard for him. There is no marital violation or offense that cannot be overcome with His supernatural intervention. However, He will NOT override anyone's will to make their marriage work. Both people must be willing to lay their hearts before God and surrender themselves to the unequivocal path He lays for the restoration, or should I say renewal, of their marriage.

But if one or both parties decide that they are justified in their slight, and will not bend to resolve a marital issue(s), then divorce is the ultimate resolution and has been allowed by God, via a bill of divorce. The hope, however, is not that the divorced parties leave the courtroom with a mindset of "Next" but a broken spirit and repentant heart, seeking the Father's forgiveness and guidance for individual restoration. Prayerfully, each person will seek the Lord to open the eyes of their understanding to THEIR role in the demise of the marriage, healing for those deficiencies, and wisdom concerning how to love themselves, others, and a future mate, (if they still desire to do so).

Therefore, instead of filling the remainder of this section with condemning scriptures about adultery, and a divorced person's imprisonment with their former mate until they die — barring certain exceptions — I will list the scriptures that speak to God's redeeming nature for any SIN and His promise to restore us and establish our path when we repent and turn to Him.

Divorce

I acknowledged my sin to you, and I did not cover my iniquity; I said, "I will confess my transgressions to the Lord," and you forgave the iniquity of my sin. Selah. Psalm 32:5

If my people who are called by my name humble themselves, and pray and seek my face and turn from their wicked ways, then I will hear from heaven and will forgive their sin and heal their land. 2 Chronicles 7:14

There is therefore now no condemnation for those who are in Christ Jesus. For the law of the Spirit of life has set you free in Christ Jesus from the law of sin and death. For God has done what the law, weakened by the flesh, could not do. By sending his own Son in the likeness of sinful flesh and for sin, he condemned sin in the flesh, in order that the righteous requirement of the law might be fulfilled in us, who walk not according to the flesh but according to the Spirit. Romans 8:1-4

Remember not the former things, nor consider the things of old. Behold, I am doing a new thing; now it springs forth, do you not perceive it? I will make a way in the wilderness and rivers in the desert.
Isaiah 43:18-19

Brothers, I do not consider that I have made it my own. But one thing I do: forgetting what lies behind and straining forward to what lies ahead, I press on toward the goal for the prize of the upward call of God in Christ Jesus. Philippians 3:13-14

And we know that God causes all things to work together for good to those who love God, to those who are called according to His purpose. Romans 8:28 NASB

A Prayer for Healing Following Divorce
Adopted and modified from -Mountain Streams Healing Center

This prayer should be said as part of your daily prayer and worship time before the Father. Additionally, this powerful affirmation should be repeated whenever negative feelings for your former spouse arise:
"I bless you with love, and I release you. You are free, and I am free."

"Lord, today I come to you with a broken heart. My relationship has ended with my spouse. I never thought it would happen to me. It happens to others, but I never dreamed I would be there one day. Lord, today I offer you all the broken pieces of my heart, my soul, my body, and my mind, and humbly ask that you heal me.

Lord, I feel tired, hurt, angry, bitter, and confused. Please take me in your arms and rock me like a baby. Soothe my heart, heal my mind and emotions. Lord, please touch every part of me that aches. Bathe me in your Balm of Gilead. Let your healing touch flow to the innermost part of my wounds. Don't let this anger and bitterness grow. Replace them with joy, peace, and comfort.

Lord, it is so hard for me to trust. But Lord, you have never left me, betrayed me, nor forsaken me. In time Lord, help me to begin to trust others. Send people into my life that will honor me, encourage me, and help me walk this new path that I am on. Be the Lover of my soul. Be my friend. Be my hope. Be my strength. Be my sustenance. Be my daily bread. When I am alone, comfort me. When I am tired, strengthen me.

Lord, I feel like I can't forgive, but I am willing, as I too need your forgiveness for my role in the demise of our marriage. I allow your love and forgiveness to flow through me. I am willing to be a channel of your mercy and grace. Lord, you know my needs – physical, financial, and spiritual. Give me all the riches of you. Let me never feel empty."
In Jesus' name I pray. And it is so.

Reflections on Faith (Unwavering)

This reflection was written by someone who is not only a minister, but also a spiritual father to many, and a friend. In November 2019, after a Tuesday night bible study, Minister Reggie came back to the greenroom to share a word he received concerning the praise team. I was one of the worship leaders that night and was blessed to be present.

At first, I was excited until he began speaking about the spirit of heaviness he felt coming from the stage during service. He then encouraged us to press into God's leading and "go hard" in pursuit of Him, and anything else He was leading us to do, until the end of the year. After hearing his words, my excitement was restored because it confirmed the word I received from my mother just the day before. Her instruction required my commitment to pray for a particular person for 30 days straight — without wavering — which I agreed to do.

As I was leaving, he and I crossed paths, and I told him about that mandate, specifically "not wavering." He then asked, "Do you know what it means to not waver?" I believe I gave him a drawn-out response, which was, in short, "to keep believing no matter what." After patiently listening to my definition, he responded with a profound response that has continued to bless me in my faith-walk with God to this day.

Instead of rewriting what he shared, I reached out to him and asked if he would write this reflection. I am so grateful that he humbly obliged, and I pray it will be as much a blessing to you as it was to me.

Unwavering Faith - Produced through Fire
By Min Reggie Alvarez

Pure gold put in the fire comes out of it proved pure; genuine faith put through this suffering comes out proved genuine. When Jesus wraps this all up, it's your faith, not your gold, that God will have on display as evidence of his victory. 1 Peter 1:3-9 MSG

61

If we are thrown into the blazing furnace, the God we serve is able to deliver us from it, and he will deliver us from Your Majesty's hand. But even if he does not, we want you to know, Your Majesty, that we will not serve your gods or worship the image of gold you have set up. Daniel 3:17-18 NIV

How do I know if my faith is authentic like that of Peter, who was one of the 12 disciples of Christ and unwavering like that of Shadrach, Meshach, and Abednego, the three Hebrew boys in the book of Daniel? What brought them to that place that even when they were in the very crucible of crisis, in the very center of suffering, they would not turn away from God or renounce their faith?

Well, if we look closely at Peter's walk, who was the leading disciple of Jesus, you will find that he knew first-hand about the highs and lows of the Christian life like no other disciple. You will find that Peter was the one who walked on water because of the faith he placed in Christ; but he also almost drowned, a few steps later, because his faith was still small, as Jesus would point out in Matthew 8:26.

When Peter thought his faith was strong enough to never deny Jesus, it was Christ who forecasted and told Peter that he would indeed deny Him three times...which he did. And it was Peter who was the only one to be rebuked by Jesus with these words, "Get behind me Satan," and then told that he was still setting his mind on human concerns rather than the things of God.

When we look closely at all these different trials that Peter went through in his life, we can find ourselves in most, if not all, of his experiences...right? We can confess easily enough that there were times when our faith was small and feeble in certain situations, and if we can really be honest....there may have been times when many of us even denied Christ in certain circumstances within the course of our own lives. But I have discovered this incredible truth: that all of what we went through (and maybe presently going through) concerning our faith, is part of the process of developing an unwavering faith.

You see, when Peter talks about the trials, sorrows, and sufferings that we will experience in this Christian life...it is because all that he went through; the challenges he faced in the storms, the denial of Christ, the rebuke he received, was all a part of his development. In fact, it was Jesus who said to Peter in Luke 22:31, 32, "Simon, Simon, Satan has asked to sift all of you as wheat. But I have prayed for you, Simon, that your faith may not fail. And when you have turned back, strengthen your brothers." To be sifted as wheat meant that Peter would go through great suffering. Why? Because of the value of his faith. Your faith is of incredible value. And Peter's faith was so valuable that Jesus allowed it to be tested by fire. That is why Jesus did not keep Satan from sifting Peter, but instead, interceded through prayer that Peter would not only overcome but that he would strengthen others.

That is what we find Peter doing in the letters he wrote—encouraging believers through what he learned by trial and fire.

He encourages us in 2 Peter 1:5:2-8 with these words:

"Grace and peace be yours in abundance through the knowledge of God and of Jesus our Lord. His divine power has given us everything we need for a godly life through our knowledge of him who called us by his own glory and goodness. Through these, he has given us his very great and precious promises, so

63

that through them you may participate in the divine nature, having escaped the corruption in the world caused by evil desires. For this very reason, make every effort to add to your faith goodness; and to goodness, knowledge; and to knowledge, self-control; and to self-control, perseverance; and to perseverance, godliness; and to godliness, mutual affection; and to mutual affection, love. For if you possess these qualities in increasing measure, they will keep you from being ineffective and unproductive in your knowledge of our Lord Jesus Christ."

Peter is sharing the elements that helped develop his faith. These are the things he learned through his personal failures and struggles. But there is a deeper reason why God allowed Peter to go through those trials, the same reason he allows us to go through ours. And let me share this in hopes that it does not shock you. It is not just to give us a faith that will move mountains, although that is one of the promises of faith in Matthew 21:21. And it is not just to receive whatever it is we ask for, though it is a promise of faith in Matthew 21:22. But here is the reason in which Peter describes in 1 Peter 1:7, "These have come so that the proven genuineness of your faith—of greater worth than gold, which perishes even though refined by fire—may result in praise, glory, and honor when Jesus Christ is revealed." Every trial we go through…is meant to bring us to a place where we can give God praise, glory, and honor….check this out…NO MATTER THE OUTCOME!!!!

If you should move a mountain because of your faith…GREAT…give God praise!!! If you should receive what you prayed for; a new home, a new job, a new car, an awesome marriage, a beautiful family, a healthy financial portfolio…AWESOME…praise

God!!!! But if you are in a season of difficulty, a season of dryness, and disappointment; a season, maybe of loss, hurt, shattered dreams, unanswered questions or unanswered prayer, sickness, loneliness, fear...and you can still give God glory and honor, and still believe God through it all...that is unwavering faith.

It is that unwavering faith that we find in the three Hebrews boys, Shadrach, Meshach, and Abednego, when they made this most profound statement in Daniel 3 after being threatened to be thrown into a fiery furnace, "The God we serve is able to deliver us from it, and He will deliver us from Your Majesty's hand. BUT EVEN IF HE DOES NOT, we want you to know, Your Majesty, that we will not serve your gods or worship the image of gold you have set up" (Daniel 3:17-18 NIV). It did not matter to the three friends if God delivered them or left them...they would still give Him glory and honor and remain steadfast in their values because the reward of faith is God.

It is the apostle Paul who wrote in 2 Corinthians 3-6, "All praise to God, the Father of our Lord Jesus Christ. God is our merciful Father and the source of all comfort. He comforts us in all our troubles so that we can comfort others. When they are troubled, we will be able to give them the same comfort God has given us. For the more we suffer for Christ, the more God will shower us with his comfort through Christ. Even when we are weighed down with troubles, it is for your comfort and salvation! For when we ourselves are comforted, we will certainly comfort you. Then you can patiently endure the same things we suffer."

I have met countless Christians in hospitals...young and old...who being terminally ill...would still rejoice and give God glory. It did not matter the outcome of their condition...they maintained a faith so powerful that it would bring salvation to nurses and doctors who were caring for them.

So I encourage you if you are in the very crucible of a crisis…if you are in the very center of suffering, trust that God is with You in the furnace and know that despite the outcome…you will come out as pure gold with unwavering faith.

Faith

And whatever you ask in prayer, you will receive, if you have faith." Matthew 21:22

And Jesus answered them, "Have faith in God. Truly, I say to you, whoever says to this mountain, 'Be taken up and thrown into the sea,' and does not doubt in his heart, but believes that what he says will come to pass, it will be done for him. Therefore I tell you, whatever you ask in prayer, believe that you have received it, and it will be yours. Mark 11:22-24

"For nothing will be impossible with God." Luke 1:37

So faith comes from hearing and hearing through the word of Christ. Romans 10:17

For we walk by faith, not by sight. 2 Corinthians 5:7

"But my righteous one shall live by faith, and if he shrinks back, my soul has no pleasure in him." Hebrews 10:38

Now faith is the assurance of things hoped for, the conviction of things not seen. Hebrews 11:1

And without faith it is impossible to please him, for whoever would draw near to God must believe that he exists and that he rewards those who seek him. Hebrews 11:6

But let him ask in faith, with no doubting, for the one who doubts is like a wave of the sea that is driven and tossed by the wind. James 1:6

You believe that God is one; you do well. Even the demons believe—and shudder! James 2:19

What use is it, my brethren, if someone says he has faith, but he has no works? Can that faith save him? 15 If a brother or sister is without clothing and in need of daily food, 16 and one of you says to them, "Go in peace, be warmed and be filled," and yet you do not give them what is necessary for their body, what use is that? 17 Even so, faith, if it has no works, is dead, being by itself. 18 But someone may well say, "You have faith, and I have works; show me your faith without the works, and I will show you my faith by my works." James 2:14-18 NASB

Fasting

"Yet even now," declares the Lord, "return to me with all your heart, with fasting, with weeping, and with mourning; and rend your hearts and not your garments." Return to the Lord your God, for he is gracious and merciful, slow to anger, and abounding in steadfast love; and he relents over disaster. Joel 2:12-13

Then Jesus was led up by the Spirit into the wilderness to be tempted by the devil. And after fasting forty days and forty nights, he was hungry. And the tempter came and said to him, "If you are the Son of God, command these stones to become loaves of bread." But he answered, "It is written, Man shall not live by bread alone, but by every word that comes from the mouth of God." Matthew 4:1-4

"And when you fast, do not look gloomy like the hypocrites, for they disfigure their faces that their fasting may be seen by others. Truly, I say to you; they have received their reward. But when you fast, anoint your head and wash your face, that your fasting may not be seen by others but by your Father who is in secret. And your Father who sees in secret will reward you. Matthew 6:16-18

Do not deprive one another *(sexually in marriage),* except perhaps by agreement for a limited time, that you may devote yourselves to prayer; but then come together again, so that Satan may not tempt you because of your lack of self-control. 1 Corinthians 7:5

Fear

The Lord is my light and my salvation; whom shall I fear? The Lord is the stronghold of my life; of whom shall I be afraid? When evildoers assail me to eat up my flesh, my adversaries and foes, it is they who stumble and fall. Though an army encamp against me, my heart shall not fear; though war arise against me, yet I will be confident. Psalm 27:1-3

When I am afraid, I put my trust in you. Psalm 56:3

The fear of the Lord is the beginning of wisdom; all those who practice it have a good understanding. His praise endures forever! Psalm 111:10

The Lord is on my side; I will not fear. What can man do to me?
Psalm 118:6

The fear of the Lord is a fountain of life, that one may turn away from the snares of death. Proverbs 14:27

But now thus says the Lord, he who created you, O Jacob, he who formed you, O Israel: "Fear not, for I have redeemed you; I have called you by name, you are mine. Isaiah 43:1

You came near when I called on you; you said, 'Do not fear!' Lamentations 3:57

"So have no fear of them, for nothing is covered that will not be revealed, or hidden that will not be known." Matthew 10:26

And do not fear those who kill the body but cannot kill the soul. Rather fear him who can destroy both soul and body in hell. Matthew 10:28

Behold, I have given you authority to tread on serpents and scorpions, and over all the power of the enemy, and nothing shall hurt you. Luke 10:19

What then shall we say to these things? If God is for us, who is against us? 32 He who did not spare His own Son, but delivered Him over for us all, how will He not also with Him freely give us all things? 33 Who will bring a charge against God's elect? God is the one who justifies; 34 who is the one who condemns? Christ Jesus is He who died, yes, rather who was raised, who is at the right hand of God, who also intercedes for us. 35 Who will separate us from the love of Christ? Will tribulation, or distress, or persecution, or famine, or nakedness, or peril, or sword? Romans 8:31-35 NASB

For this reason, I remind you to fan into flame the gift of God, which is in you through the laying on of my hands, for God gave us a spirit not of fear but of power and love and self-control. 2 Timothy 1:6-7

There is no fear in love, but perfect love casts out fear. For fear has to do with punishment, and whoever fears has not been perfected in love. 1 John 4:18

Reflections on Divine (True) Forgiveness

The bible teaches us that if we do not forgive, our Father in heaven will not forgive us (Matthew 6:15). So, what exactly is forgiveness? The general consensus I found via a quick Google search and personal experience is letting those who have offended you go or not holding the offense against them. However, most of the world's definition came with the caveat that one should not *forget* the offense, in order to protect themselves from further injury.

Although the part about not forgetting seems reasonable, given our human nature to protect ourselves, it is not in alignment with God's word. Ephesians 4:32 instructs us to do the following:

"Be kind to one another, tenderhearted, forgiving one another, as God in Christ forgave you."

When the word teaches us about "how" God forgives, it then says:

"I, I am he who blots out your transgressions for my own sake, and I will not remember your sins. Isaiah 43:25

"For I will be merciful toward their iniquities, and I will remember their sins no more." Hebrews 8:12

He will again have compassion on us; he will tread our iniquities underfoot. You will cast all our sins into the depths of the sea. Micah 7:19

There are plenty more scriptures from the Old to the New Testament that speak of God "forgetting" when He forgives us. So, why is it that our society allows for the "forgiving" an offense, but not "forgetting," when it comes to our forgiveness of others? Especially, when upon begging for God's forgiveness, we are also hoping that he completely lets our offense toward Him, and/or others, completely go.

Well, once again, and personally speaking, I believe that it is due to our fear that we will be wronged, hurt, used, or abused by that person again. But, believers don't have a Spirit of fear, right? I mean, aren't we called to walk by faith and not by sight or our perceptions? And– if we are always on guard for that person to hurt us again, can they ever truly be redeemed in our eyes?

In consideration of the aforementioned questions I struggled with before God opened the eyes of my understanding, I'd like to offer the following. Once you truly learn something beneficial, it is very hard to unlearn it and perform that function in a way that disadvantaged you in the past. For example, once you truly learn how to eat properly and experience the benefits of your new habits, it's difficult to go back to a lifestyle that left you sick, drained, and feeling bad about yourself.

The same can be said for learning how to love (i.e., accept) people. Once you learn that real love is not about trying to either change someone or bend and twist yourself inside out like a pretzel to be accepted by someone, you will become immune to all hurt and resentment brought about through the action of another. Why? Because true acceptance doesn't resist or manipulate; rather, it accepts and shows mercy. And please, let me be clear about the word "accept." It means to accept the information you've learned about that person and decide whether to engage, and then connect, or simply disengage and continue to walk your path without criticism or condemnation of that person and the way they CHOOSE to live THEIR life.

It is not casting judgment on their lifestyle choices as being either good or bad, but rather deciding if those choices or ways of being are complementary to yours. If not, you "accept" their decision to live as they please— absent your presence. If they behave in a way that is offensive or disrespectful to your person or ways of being, you "accept" that those behaviors are rooted in the person they are "right now" forgive the offense and disengage so that you can continue on your path. If they have actually sinned against you, you should confront them, with love, privately. If your issue is merely a difference in lifestyle choices, you can again "accept" that they are walking a path or hold beliefs that are different from yours, and without judgment, choose to move forward.

There may also be times that God leads you to pray for that person. However, you will not be *willing* to pray for them, at least not with an open and non-judgmental spirit, if you are holding an offense against them. There are two ways we can obey God, willingly and unwillingly. However, the blessing comes when we serve or give "willingly", not grudgingly or out of necessity, as God loves a cheerful giver (and that doesn't just apply to money). One cannot sincerely pray goodwill toward someone they are harboring bitterness towards. Nor can one willingly and with an open heart obey God, if they are rebelling against Him in favor of their own desires. They must surrender their will to His way, willingly, and if they can't, pray that God will give them a willing heart. Disobeying God's leading is sin, and it only leads to torment, not to mention cutting yourself off from the blessing He is trying to give you through your obedience.

In closing, I'd like to ask you this question: Have you ever done something to someone, or believed something to be a fact, only to realize your offense or that you were wrong – years, or months, and sometimes

DAYS later? This has happened to me several times and was the impetus for me really starting to search certain themes out in the scripture for a better understanding.

There are times when I behaved in a way that was hurtful to others (being critical, bossy, impatient, self-righteous, insensitive, etc. – I mean I could go on all day), and I believed I was in the right because of their actions. However, it is NEVER okay to behave in a disrespectful way toward others. When the eyes of my understanding were opened, I wished I could go back and "make things right." Sometimes I could, and sometimes I couldn't. Sometimes I did, but the person didn't really believe I changed. Nonetheless, the fact remained that at the time of my offense, I really wasn't aware, at least not on a conscious level, that my actions were wrong or offensive.

That is when I got a true understanding of Jesus' prayer on the cross, in Luke 23:34, "Father, forgive them, for they do not know what they are doing". Even if a person walked up to you and spat in your face, the fact that they could do such a thing to another human being shows that they are not fully aware of just how offensive and hurtful they are being. Does that mean you forgive them and then invite them to go have coffee? No! It means you accept the truth of their actions, which communicate their inability to walk in love toward you. You then disengage and continue on your path. If you are assaulted in the manner above and provided with the opportunity to press charges, you should first consult God as far as what to do. Even if you are led to press charges due to a physical assault on your person or property, you forgive, step back, pray for that person, and that their eyes be opened to their behavior. Pray for God's mercy and continue to walk your path.

In the same way you would not personally engage a stranger, now that the slate has been wiped clean with the offender, I do not recommend personally engaging this person unless God grants neutral proximity. This person must also request and consistently demonstrate their ability to walk in love toward you. And even if that should happen, you must then evaluate if the morals, principles, and beliefs by which you both live life are complimentary before deciding to connect.

Only being led by the Holy Spirit can allow you to do that successfully, every time. Whether you decide to connect in a new way or not, you will have truly forgiven them by absolving them of the offense, AND let it go by refusing to hold it against them.

One of the things I do after forgiving someone, and I'm still struggling to release old memories connected to it, is say the following affirmation whenever it comes to mind: *I salute the Divinity in you. I see you only as God sees you, perfect, made in His image and likeness. I* bless the past with love, and I release you. You are free, and I am free.

I pray that you will be led by the Spirit in everything you do, especially concerning how to walk in love toward others, which starts with learning to truly forgive. Not just yourself, but also others, the way God has forgiven you.

Forgiveness

"I, I am he who blots out your transgressions for my own sake, and I will not remember your sins." Isaiah 43:25

Blessed are the merciful, for they shall receive mercy. Matthew 5:7

But if you do not forgive others their trespasses, neither will your Father forgive your trespasses. Matthew 6:15

Then Peter came up and said to him, "Lord, how often will my brother sin against me, and I forgive him? As many as seven times?" Jesus said to him, "I do not say to you seven times, but seventy times seven." Matthew 18:21-22

"But I say to you who hear, Love your enemies, do good to those who hate you," Luke 6:27

"Judge not, and you will not be judged; condemn not, and you will not be condemned; forgive, and you will be forgiven"; Luke 6:37

Pay attention to yourselves! If your brother sins, rebuke him, and if he repents, forgive him, and if he sins against you seven times in the day, and turns to you seven times, saying, 'I repent,' you must forgive him. Luke 17:3-4

"And whenever you stand praying, forgive, if you have anything against anyone, so that your Father also who is in heaven may forgive you your trespasses." Mark 11:25

Repay no one evil for evil, but give thought to do what is honorable in the sight of all. Romans 12:17

Let all bitterness and wrath and anger and clamor and slander be put away from you, along with all malice. Be kind to one another, tenderhearted, forgiving one another, as God in Christ forgave you. Ephesians 4:31-32

Bearing with one another and, if one has a complaint against another, forgiving each other; as the Lord has forgiven you, so you also must forgive. Colossians 3:13

If we confess our sins, he is faithful and just to forgive us our sins and to cleanse us from all unrighteousness. If we say we have not sinned, we make him a liar, and his word is not in us. 1 John 1:9-10

Affirmations for Divine Forgiveness

I am now immune to all hurt and resentment. My poise is built upon a rock – the Christ within.

I always call on the law of forgiveness by forgiving any offense and quickly letting it go. I salute the Divinity in my neighbors, I speak that I see them only as God sees them; perfect and made in His image and likeness. I bless the past with love, and I let it go!

(Offender Name) I bless you with love, and I release you! You are free, and I am free! *Say this affirmation whenever thoughts of the offender and/or offense come to mind.*

I bless the past with love, and let it go, fully living and rejoicing in the present, and trusting the future and all it holds to the Father.

I always call on the law of forgiveness by forgiving any offense, and quickly letting it go. I salute the Divinity in my brothers and sisters, I speak that I see them only as God sees them; perfect and made in His image and likeness. I bless the past with love, and let it go.

Yesterday is truly gone, and the only things that can be saved are things that are good, true, and of real love, for those are the only things that can live in one's heart and give life to the soul, thereby restoring it to its God state. All things of material and negative nature, fear, bitterness, and resentment must be left behind.

I bless you and bless you with the rich substance of God's love.

Reflections on Giving

"Give, and it will be given to you. They will pour into your lap a good measure-- pressed down, shaken together, and running over. For by your standard of measure it will be measured to you in return." Luke 6:38 NASB

In all my years of church attendance, I would have to say that the most preached topic has been giving. Be it through giving money or using your talents in ministry service, or simply giving time – giving money always seemed to be the most important of the three. The amount and frequency in which I gave were also taught to be the metric used to determine how blessed I was, or could be. And that's how it was.

At one time in my life, I endured years of hearing Malachi 3:8-9, admonishing me that I would be "cursed with a curse" if I didn't tithe. Questioning why I wasn't required to do ANY other part of the Mosaic Law was not allowed, as was questioning why we were not tithing according to the way the Children of Israel tithed in the Old Testament. Not to mention the fact that New Testament believers were under a new covenant and therefore instructed to give according to how they purposed in their heart (2 Corinthians 9:7), not "grudgingly or of necessity," which is how some of us were giving.

It wasn't until I finally left the church in which I was subject to this requirement and began researching this topic for myself that I came into an understanding concerning how I should give. When I went back to my former church equipped with the knowledge to again question the practice and demand a response, I was told that tithing was done before the law, and was therefore applicable after. That particular Pastor also told me that if he told people they didn't have to tithe, "there would only be a dollar in the offering plate." Wow!

It was at this moment that I realized he'd been pushing this requirement for so many years out of fear that God would not provide. I was also grateful that God had released me from that ministry, and would pray for them at times when they came to mind.

I share that experience with you because, like myself so many years ago, I know that there are people who are under bondage to that teaching. Jesus said in Matthew 11:30 that His yoke is easy, and His burden is light. He also admonished spiritual leaders against heaping burdens on people while not lifting a finger to lighten their load (Luke 11:46), and Paul admonished in Galatians 5:3 that if we attempt to be justified by any part of the law, then we are cursed and have fallen away from grace.

Now, does that mean we should not tithe at all? No. It means that it is your CHOICE to give a tenth, or a half, or nothing at all. There is no curse or great consequence that will befall you if you do not tithe. However, the blessings that accompany tithing from a cheerful heart are still in effect and will apply if you do, just as they did before the Law of Tithing came into effect.

In 2 Corinthian 9:6-8, Paul taught the following:

Now, this I say, he who sows sparingly will also reap sparingly, and he who sows bountifully will also reap bountifully. 7Each one must do just as he has purposed in his heart, not grudgingly or under compulsion, for God loves a cheerful giver. 8And God is able to make all grace abound to you, so that always having all sufficiency in everything, you may have an abundance for every good deed;

The same applies to believers in the Body of Christ today, whether it is a tithe (tenth), a penny, or any other amount. However, just as in the instances of Jacob tithing before the Law of Moses (Genesis 28:20), there is certainly a blessing that accompanies one who commits in his heart to give a tithe to God in appreciation for His protection, provision, and peace. There are many people who possess great wealth, but they are obsessed with protecting it and themselves because of it, not to mention devising schemes and plans to maintain it, and therefore have no peace.

God does not desire for us to love money to the point where it manifests evil in our lives (1 Timothy 6:10). He also doesn't desire for us to be so burdened down with trying to pay tithes or any other financial obligations to Him, that we neglect our civic (Matthew 22:21) and family obligations (1 Timothy 5:8). The tithing law itself required paying the "tenth part" of one's harvest or cattle increase, which means living off the first nine pieces of livestock or 90 percent of grain, oil, and wine, and giving God the tenth– not giving away the first 10 percent and having nothing to live off and grow.

Of course, I am aware that we are no longer in biblical times and that our universal means of currency is money. However, that only further supports why tithing, according to Mosaic Law, is not possible in practice or purpose today, according to Mosaic Law.

If you have been struggling to understand or grudgingly fulfill the Law of Tithing, it is my prayer that you would now be released to give freely and receive God's grace concerning your finances. When I finally learned the truth about tithing and started using the money God blessed me with to first care for the needs of my household (unless when led otherwise) and then prioritizing other financial obligations, I was then able to truly give freely, and with greater abundance. I also believe that God, seeing my desire to tithe, and give even more than a tenth of my wealth, supernaturally blessed me by increasing my finances, providing opportunities for debts to be cleared, contractual obligations to be voided, various properties to be legally acquired with no financial reserves, and so much more.

Want to take giving one step further? Continue to give as God leads, but also endeavor to speak God's word in 2 Corinthians 9:10, where He promised to give seed to the sower. Because having seed to sow requires an increase beyond essential needs. Give, and it WILL be given unto you, good measure pressed down, shaken together, and running over will men GIVE into your lap (Luke 6:38). I've been a recipient of this promise many times over by sowing into good ground as well as toward people and projects in obedience to God's leading. Therefore, I can affirm that *God is my instant, constant, and abundant supply. I am a sower with ample seeds to sow. I am blessed to be a blessing in every way, including gifts, talents, abilities, and treasures.* And it is so!

Giving (Freewill - Tithing - Service)

Honor the Lord with your wealth and with the firstfruits of all your produce; then your barns will be filled with plenty, and your vats will be bursting with wine. Proverbs 3:9-10

Do not withhold good from those to whom it is due, when it is in your power to do it. Proverbs 3:27

Whoever is generous to the poor lends to the Lord, and he will repay him for his deed. Proverbs 19:17

Beware of practicing your righteousness before other people in order to be seen by them, for then you will have no reward from your Father who is in heaven. Thus, when you give to the needy, sound no trumpet before you, as the hypocrites do in the synagogues and in the streets, that they may be praised by others. Truly, I say to you, they have received their reward. But when you give to the needy, do not let your left hand know what your right hand is doing, so that your giving may be in secret. And your Father who sees in secret will reward you. Matthew 6:1-4

For where your treasure is, there your heart will be also. Matthew 6:21

Give to everyone who begs from you, and from one who takes away your goods do not demand them back. Luke 6:30

Give, and it will be given to you. Good measure, pressed down, shaken together, running over, will be put into your lap. For with the measure you use it will be measured back to you. Luke 6:38

In all things I have shown you that by working hard in this way we must help the weak and remember the words of the Lord Jesus, how he himself said, 'It is more blessed to give than to receive.' Acts 20:35

The point is this: whoever sows sparingly will also reap sparingly, and whoever sows bountifully will also reap bountifully. 7 Each one must give as he has decided in his heart, not reluctantly or under compulsion, for God loves a cheerful giver. 2 Corinthians 9:7

He who supplies seed to the sower and bread for food will supply and multiply your seed for sowing and increase the harvest of your righteousness. 2 Corinthians 9:10

Do not neglect to do good and to share what you have, for such sacrifices are pleasing to God. Hebrews 13:16

Gluttony

When you sit down to eat with a ruler, observe carefully what is before you, and put a knife to your throat if you are given to appetite. Do not desire his delicacies, for they are deceptive food. Proverbs 23:1-3

For the drunkard and the glutton will come to poverty, and slumber will clothe them with rags. Proverbs 23:21

If you have found honey, eat only enough for you, lest you have your fill of it and vomit it. Proverbs 25:16

But he answered, "It is written, Man shall not live by bread alone, but by every word that comes from the mouth of God." Matthew 4:4

But put on the Lord Jesus Christ, and make no provision for the flesh, to gratify its desires. Romans 13:14

Do you not know that you are God's temple and that God's Spirit dwells in you? If anyone destroys God's temple, God will destroy him. For God's temple is holy, and you are that temple. 1 Corinthians 3:16-17

But I discipline my body and keep it under control, lest after preaching to others I myself should be disqualified. 1 Corinthians 9:27

Since we have these promises, beloved, let us cleanse ourselves from every defilement of body and spirit, bringing holiness to completion in the fear of God. 2 Corinthians 7:1

But the fruit of the Spirit is love, joy, peace, patience, kindness, goodness, faithfulness, gentleness, self-control; against such things there is no law. Galatians 5:22-23

For many, of whom I have often told you and now tell you even with tears, walk as enemies of the cross of Christ. Their end is destruction, their god is their belly, and they glory in their shame, with minds set on earthly things. Philippians 3:18-19

God (Presence – fellowship - Kingdom)

Have I not commanded you? Be strong and courageous. Do not be frightened, and do not be dismayed, for the Lord your God is with you wherever you go. Joshua 1:9

You make known to me the path of life; in your presence there is fullness of joy; at your right hand are pleasures forevermore. Psalm 16:11

Oh, how abundant is your goodness, which you have stored up for those who fear you and worked for those who take refuge in you, in the sight of the children of mankind! In the cover of your presence you hide them from the plots of men; you store them in your shelter from the strife of tongues. Psalm 31:19-20

Am I a God at hand, declares the Lord, and not a God far away? Can a man hide himself in secret places so that I cannot see him? declares the Lord. Do I not fill heaven and earth? declares the Lord.
Jeremiah 23:23-24

For where two or three are gathered in my name, there am I among them.
Matthew 18:20

I am the vine; you are the branches. Whoever abides in me and I in him, he it is that bears much fruit, for apart from me you can do nothing.
John 15:5

Teaching them to observe all that I have commanded you. And behold, I am with you always, to the end of the age. Matthew 28:20

Keep your life free from love of money, and be content with what you have, for he has said, "I will never leave you nor forsake you." Hebrews 13:5

Draw near to God, and he will draw near to you. Cleanse your hands, you sinners, and purify your hearts, you double-minded. James 4:8

Guidance

Seek the Lord and his strength; seek his presence continually! 1 Chronicles 16:11

Make me to know your ways, O Lord; teach me your paths. Lead me in your truth and teach me, for you are the God of my salvation; for you I wait all the day long. Psalm 25:4-5

He leads the humble in what is right, and teaches the humble his way. All the paths of the Lord are steadfast love and faithfulness, for those who keep his covenant and his testimonies. Psalm 25:9-10

The steps of a man are established by the Lord, when he delights in his way; though he fall, he shall not be cast headlong, for the Lord upholds his hand. Psalm 37:23-24

How can a young man keep his way pure? By guarding it according to your word. Psalm 119:9

Your word is a lamp to my feet and a light to my path. Psalm 119:105
Let me hear in the morning of your steadfast love, for in you I trust. Make me know the way I should go, for to you I lift up my soul. Psalm 143:8

Trust in the Lord with all your heart, and do not lean on your own understanding. In all your ways acknowledge him, and he will make straight your paths. Proverbs 3:5-6

Where there is no guidance, a people falls, but in an abundance of counselors there is safety. Proverbs 11:14

The heart of man plans his way, but the Lord establishes his steps. Proverbs 16:9

Thus says the Lord, your Redeemer, the Holy One of Israel: "I am the Lord your God, who teaches you to profit, who leads you in the way you should go. Isaiah 48:17

And the Lord will guide you continually and satisfy your desire in scorched places and make your bones strong; and you shall be like a watered garden, like a spring of water, whose waters do not fail. Isaiah 58:11

When the Spirit of truth comes, he will guide you into all the truth, for he will not speak on his own authority, but whatever he hears he will speak, and he will declare to you the things that are to come. John 16:13

I can do nothing on my own. As I hear, I judge, and my judgment is just, because I seek not my own will but the will of him who sent me. John 5:30

Reflections on Healing

I really dragged my feet on this reflection and the Reflection on Divine Prosperity, because these are both very touchy subjects in the Body of Christ. However, after going back and forth with God about the time it would take, and His Spirit continuing to lead me to write, I decided to be obedient. So here it goes!

I've seen many people pray for the healing of everything from the slightest pain to terminal illness. Some recovered, and some did not. Some managed to live with the condition, illness, or disease for the rest of their lives, and some simply died. I am sure that many of us have had similar experiences. And at some point, the same question always pops up: Why do some people get healed, while others do not? Is it a matter of faith? Is it a matter of sin? Is it a matter of God's perfect will, or a little bit of all of the above? The answer to those questions is that no one, but God, knows why some people recover from illness, and some don't.

However, maybe the question shouldn't be why someone does or does not recover, but rather why were they afflicted? 1 Peter 2:24 reads:

> "And He Himself bore our sins in His body on the cross, so that we might die to sin and live to righteousness; for by His wounds, you were healed."

I mentioned that scripture first because some believers, through the teaching of Spiritual leaders, stake their faith in God's guaranteed healing on that verse. However, the simple fact that the word states that Christ "bore our sins" on the cross that we might die to sin and live to righteousness, denotes that Christ's death provided those who believe with the *spiritual* healing of our sinful condition at that very moment. This verse could not have been speaking of physical healing, due to the

86

simple fact that it states we "were" healed at the point of His death, and the fact that from then till now, people still continue to be afflicted with all sorts of illnesses.

Various scriptures reference people being healed instantly (Acts 14:8-10 – when the Apostle Paul noticed a crippled man "who had faith to be healed" in Lystra, commanded him to stand, and he leaped and walked), and people praying for healing and not receiving it, (2 Corinthians 12:9 - Paul begging to be healed, but accepting that his affliction was being used to keep him humble, and accepting God's grace instead).

So, it can't be God's will that we NEVER get afflicted or that we are guaranteed healing. However, in accepting God's free gift of salvation, we are provided with the *opportunity* to have abundant life (John 10:10 "might have"), promised that no weapon formed against us would prosper (Isaiah 54:17), and that God would cause ALL things to work for our good (Romans 8:28). We are also taught that it is appointed unto man once to die (Hebrews 9:27), indicating that each of us will die from something (not excluding illness) at some point, unless we live to see the rapture (1 Corinthians 15).

I shared these particular verses to emphasize that all of us will, at times, experience illness/affliction of various degrees. But what sets the believer apart from those who are ignorant to the power of Christ within us, and that of our spoken word, is that while awaiting healing we can still choose to thrive and prosper in our thinking, spirits, and physical disposition, if we continue to speak life (Proverbs 18:21).

That means speaking that you are healthy, whole, and well, regardless of any symptoms your body may present, or the report of a physician. It means continuing to speak of God's ability to do the impossible (Luke 1:37), yet resting in his promise to work everything, including your affliction, for your good (Romans 8:28), and being obedient to His word to give thanks for everything, yes, even your affliction (1 Thessalonians 5:18). In doing this, God promised to keep us in perfect peace (Isaiah 26:3) and manifest His strength within us to full perfection (2 Corinthians 12:9), while supplying us with enough grace to endure any illness.

Therefore, the first place we must look when we are afflicted is within. Bring ourselves before the Father and ask Him to open the eyes of our understanding to anything we may be doing to attract and/or perpetuate the illness within us. And that goes for mental, emotional, and spiritual affliction as well. Sometimes, the truth is that we are the cause of our own affliction through harboring bitterness, anger, unforgiveness, and engaging in perpetual sin. That is not always the case, but accounts for some of the physical, emotional, and spiritual ailments many of us face. We also attract illness by harboring self-defeating thoughts and speaking abusive words to ourselves and toward others.

There are many cases where certain "dis-eases" would be totally eliminated by forgiving someone, releasing our control or illusion of control over someone's life, repenting of sinful behavior, or releasing any anger, bitterness, and any other negative emotion concerning a person or situation.

No one can harbor positive and negative thoughts simultaneously. It's not possible to walk around thinking you are smart, talented, and beautiful, while simultaneously thinking you are dumb, talentless, and ugly. At the same time, you cannot simultaneously speak words of love and appreciation toward someone while speaking words of hate and disgust. Well, you could, but they'd probably look at you like you were crazy, walk away, or attempt to have you committed! Either way, one mindset or way of speaking is sure to outweigh the other. Since it is easy to speak that you are sick, broken, and/or have a "disease" while enduring a debilitating condition (even for a short time), it takes extra effort to speak that you are healing and that God is intervening, to bring you into a state of total and complete wholeness– regardless of how you feel or what you see.

Choosing to speak life-affirming words doesn't mean that instant healing will manifest or that there will be no sign of illness, ever. Doing so might only manifest treatments to manage the symptoms, or enable you to live symptom-free the rest of your life, even though test results show an illness is still present. It may manifest total and complete healing altogether, or help you to stand as your symptoms fade over time; naturally or with treatment. Or help to extend your life six months or six years longer than the doctor estimated. However, in the time that remained, you were an example of God's supernatural grace, mercy, and power working through you as you endured. But, regardless of the outcome, what you certainly CANNOT do, is continue to speak that you have (insert illness). Instead, say that you are daily overcoming the symptoms and believing God for the full manifestation of your healing.

So, to put all this into context, I'd like to present this scenario. Let's say that you were afflicted with an illness, be it as a consequence of your actions or for God's purpose, or both. You petition God to be healed, and He says: "Alright. I've heard your petition, and I am going to heal you, but not right away. However, to ease your mind, I'll tell you when. He then says, "I am going to heal you in exactly three years and fifty-nine days. Until that time, I will give you the grace to endure, treatment to manage the symptoms, and my peace as you trust in my ability to keep my word." What would you say? What would you do? Would you grumble and complain, knowing that things will still be carried out that way, whether you accept it or not? Or, would you rejoice in knowing that God sees and hears you, and is able to heal you in His time, or sooner if the affliction can be resolved by direct action on your part? And until then, will you rest in the truth that He will provide you with everything you need to endure and have peace while you wait?

My prayer is that whenever you are afflicted, regardless of the why, that you choose the latter and continue to speak life, meaning the word of God concerning His power and your ability to receive His grace and mercy while you endure. That, before you claim a death sentence due to a lab result or prolonged symptoms, you bring it to Him and ask that He search you to reveal whether you are complicit in the cause, and if so, how to change. And in instances where that's not the case, receive His grace to endure and trust Him for total healing, while He uses the affliction for His purpose. Continue to thank Him for comfort, wisdom to manage the symptoms, supernatural joy in spite of, and reassurance that if "the" (not your) affliction is something He is allowing for His purpose, it will be used for His Glory, your good, and the good of others, until the fullness of your healing manifests. And it is so!

Healing (Physical and Spiritual)

If my people who are called by my name humble themselves, and pray and seek my face and turn from their wicked ways, then I will hear from heaven and will forgive their sin and heal their land. 2 Chronicles 7:14

The Lord sustains him on his sickbed; in his illness you restore him to full health. Psalm 41:3

Bless the Lord, O my soul, and forget not all his benefits, who forgives all your iniquity, who heals all your diseases, who redeems your life from the pit, who crowns you with steadfast love and mercy . . .
Psalm 103:2-4

He heals the brokenhearted and binds up their wounds. Psalm 147:3

My son, be attentive to my words; incline your ear to my sayings. Let them not escape from your sight; keep them within your heart. For they are life to those who find them, and healing to all their flesh.
Proverbs 4:20-22

But he was wounded for our transgressions; he was crushed for our iniquities; upon him was the chastisement that brought us peace, and with his stripes we are healed. Isaiah 53:5

Heal me, O Lord, and I shall be healed; save me, and I shall be saved, for you are my praise. Jeremiah 17:14

Behold, I will bring to it health and healing, and I will heal them and reveal to them abundance of prosperity and security. Jeremiah 33:6

Is anyone among you sick? Let him call for the elders of the church, and let them pray over him, anointing him with oil in the name of the Lord. And the prayer of faith will save the one who is sick, and the Lord will raise him up. And if he has committed sins, he will be forgiven.
James 5:14-15

Therefore, confess your sins to one another and pray for one another, that you may be healed. The prayer of a righteous person has great power as it is working. James 5:16

He himself bore our sins in his body on the tree, that we might die to sin and live to righteousness. By his wounds, you have been healed.
1 Peter 2:24

Beloved, I pray that all may go well with you and that you may be in good health, as it goes well with your soul. 3 John 1:2

Affirmations for Divine Healing

Divine love now dissolves and dissipates every wrong condition in my mind, body, and affairs. Divine love is the most powerful chemical in the universe and dissolves everything that is not of itself.

I am being healed with God's help. Praise God, I am healed in body, mind, and spirit.

All barriers and obstacles to my divinely given good, health, and healing are now dissolved with God's help.

Infinite and Divine Spirit, I thank You that I am complete and in Divine order. Yes – I and all my affairs are in Divine order, and I walk in Divine health, wealth, love, and perfect self-expression.

Hindrances – Prayer/Blessings/Christian Walk

If I had cherished iniquity in my heart, the Lord would not have listened.
Psalm 66:18

But your iniquities have made a separation between you and your God, and your sins have hidden his face from you so that he does not hear.
Isaiah 59:2

Enter by the narrow gate. For the gate is wide and the way is easy that leads to destruction, and those who enter by it are many. For the gate is narrow and the way is hard that leads to life, and those who find it are few. Matthew 7:13-14

Therefore let us not pass judgment on one another any longer, but rather decide never to put a stumbling block or hindrance in the way of a brother. Romans 14:13

I appeal to you, brothers, to watch out for those who cause divisions and create obstacles contrary to the doctrine that you have been taught; avoid them. Romans 16:17

Therefore, since we are surrounded by so great a cloud of witnesses, let us also lay aside every weight, and sin which clings so closely, and let us run with endurance the race that is set before us, Hebrews 12:1

You ask and do not receive, because you ask wrongly, to spend it on your passions. James 4:3

Intercession

But I say to you, Love your enemies and pray for those who persecute you, Matthew 5:44

Likewise the Spirit helps us in our weakness. For we do not know what to pray for as we ought, but the Spirit himself intercedes for us with groanings too deep for words. And he who searches hearts knows what is the mind of the Spirit, because the Spirit intercedes for the saints according to the will of God. Romans 8:26-27

Who is to condemn? Christ Jesus is the one who died—more than that, who was raised—who is at the right hand of God, who indeed is interceding for us. Romans 8:34

In the days of his flesh, Jesus offered up prayers and supplications, with loud cries and tears, to him who was able to save him from death, and he was heard because of his reverence. Hebrews 5:7

Consequently, he is able to save to the uttermost those who draw near to God through him, since he always lives to make intercession for them. Hebrews 7:25

First of all, then, I urge that supplications, prayers, intercessions, and thanksgivings be made for all people, for kings and all who are in high positions, that we may lead a peaceful and quiet life, godly and dignified in every way. This is good, and it is pleasing in the sight of God our Savior, who desires all people to be saved and to come to the knowledge of the truth. For there is one God, and there is one mediator between God and men, the man Christ Jesus . . . 1 Timothy 2:1-5

Judgment (Godly Vs. Ungodly)

Do not judge so that you will not be judged. 2 For in the way you judge, you will be judged; and by your standard of measure, it will be measured to you. 3 Why do you look at the speck that is in your brother's eye, but do not notice the log that is in your own eye? 4 Or how can you say to your brother, 'Let me take the speck out of your eye,' and behold, the log is in your own eye? 5 You hypocrite, first take the log out of your own eye, and then you will see clearly to take the speck out of your brother's eye. Matthew 7:1-5 NASB

"For by your words you will be justified, and by your words you will be condemned." Matthew 12:37

Judge not, and you will not be judged; condemn not, and you will not be condemned; forgive, and you will be forgiven; Luke 6:37

Do not judge by appearances, but judge with right judgment. John 7:24

Therefore you have no excuse, O man, every one of you who judges. For in passing judgment on another you condemn yourself, because you, the judge, practice the very same things. Romans 2:1

But because of your stubbornness and unrepentant heart you are storing up wrath for yourself in the day of wrath and revelation of the righteous judgment of God, 6 who will render to each person according to his deeds: 7 to those who by perseverance in doing good seek for glory and honor and immortality, eternal life; 8 but to those who are selfishly ambitious and do not obey the truth, but obey unrighteousness, wrath and indignation. 9 There will be tribulation and distress for every soul of man who does evil, of the Jew first and also of the Greek, 10 but glory and honor and peace to everyone who does good, to the Jew first and also to the Greek. 11 For there is no partiality with God. Romans 2:5-11 NASB

Why do you pass judgment on your brother? Or you, why do you despise your brother? For we will all stand before the judgment seat of God; for it is written, "As I live, says the Lord, every knee shall bow to me, and every tongue shall confess to God." So then each of us will give an account of himself to God. Romans 14:10-12

For we must all appear before the judgment seat of Christ, so that each one may receive what is due for what he has done in the body, whether good or evil. 2 Corinthians 5:10

My brethren, do not hold your faith in our glorious Lord Jesus Christ with an attitude of personal favoritism. 2 For if a man comes into your assembly with a gold ring and dressed in fine clothes, and there also comes in a poor man in dirty clothes, 3 and you pay special attention to

the one who is wearing the fine clothes, and say, "You sit here in a good place," and you say to the poor man, "You stand over there, or sit down by my footstool," 4 have you not made distinctions among yourselves, and become judges with evil motives? 5 Listen, my beloved brethren: did not God choose the poor of this world to be rich in faith and heirs of the kingdom which He promised to those who love Him?
James 2:1-5 NASB

For judgment is without mercy to one who has shown no mercy. Mercy triumphs over judgment. James 2:13

Justice (Vengeance)

Turn away from evil and do good; so shall you dwell forever. For the Lord loves justice; he will not forsake his saints. They are preserved forever, but the children of the wicked shall be cut off. The righteous shall inherit the land and dwell upon it forever. Psalm 37:27-29

To do righteousness and justice is more acceptable to the Lord than sacrifice. Proverbs 21:3

When justice is done, it is a joy to the righteous but terror to evildoers Proverbs 21:15

Whoever says to the wicked, "You are in the right," will be cursed by peoples, abhorred by nations, but those who rebuke the wicked will have delight, and a good blessing will come upon them. Proverbs 24:24-25

Learn to do good; seek justice, correct oppression; bring justice to the fatherless, plead the widow's cause. Isaiah 1:17

Therefore the Lord waits to be gracious to you, and therefore he exalts himself to show mercy to you. For the Lord is a God of justice; blessed are all those who wait for him. Isaiah 30:18

He has told you, O man, what is good; and what does the Lord require of you but to do justice, and to love kindness, and to walk humbly with your God? Micah 6:8

So whatever you wish that others would do to you, do also to them, for this is the Law and the Prophets. Matthew 7:12

Repay no one evil for evil, but give thought to do what is honorable in the sight of all. If possible, so far as it depends on you, live peaceably with all. Beloved, never avenge yourselves, but leave it to the wrath of God, for it is written, "Vengeance is mine, I will repay, says the Lord." To the contrary, "if your enemy is hungry, feed him; if he is thirsty, give him something to drink; for by so doing you will heap burning coals on his head." Do not be overcome by evil, but overcome evil with good. Romans 12:17-21

For the wrongdoer will be paid back for the wrong he has done, and there is no partiality. Colossians 3:25

For we know him who said, "Vengeance is mine; I will repay." And again, "The Lord will judge his people." Hebrews 10:30

Do not repay evil for evil or reviling for reviling, but on the contrary, bless, for to this you were called, that you may obtain a blessing. For "Whoever desires to love life and see good days, let him keep his tongue from evil and his lips from speaking deceit; let him turn away from evil and do good; let him seek peace and pursue it. 1 Peter 3:9-11

Loneliness

It is the Lord who goes before you. He will be with you; he will not leave you or forsake you. Do not fear or be dismayed. Deuteronomy 31:8

For my father and my mother have forsaken me, but the Lord will take me in. Psalm 27:10

Where shall I go from your Spirit? Or where shall I flee from your presence? If I ascend to heaven, you are there! If I make my bed in Sheol, you are there! If I take the wings of the morning and dwell in the uttermost parts of the sea, even there your hand shall lead me, and your right hand shall hold me. Psalm 139:7-10

A man of many companions may come to ruin, but there is a friend who sticks closer than a brother. Proverbs 18:24

Who shall separate us from the love of Christ? Shall tribulation, or distress, or persecution, or famine, or nakedness, or danger, or sword? As it is written, "For your sake we are being killed all the day long; we are regarded as sheep to be slaughtered." No, in all these things we are more than conquerors through him who loved us. For I am sure that neither death nor life, nor angels nor rulers, nor things present nor things to come, nor powers, nor height nor depth, nor anything else in all creation, will be able to separate us from the love of God in Christ Jesus our Lord. Romans 8:35-39

At my first defense no one came to stand by me, but all deserted me. May it not be charged against them! But the Lord stood by me and strengthened me, so that through me the message might be fully proclaimed and all the Gentiles might hear it. So I was rescued from the lion's mouth. 2 Timothy 4:16-17

Reflections on Divine Love

'And you shall love the Lord your God with all your heart and with all your soul and with all your mind and with all your strength.' The second is this: 'You shall love your neighbor as yourself.' There is no other commandment greater than these. Mark 12: 30-31

Before I jump into this reflection, I want to pose this question: What does it mean to Love God with all your heart, soul, mind, and strength, and then to love yourself? I ask this question, intentionally leaving out the part about loving your neighbor, as I don't believe that to be possible unless you first know what it means, by way of first loving God and yourself.

So here's my answer, considering years of trial and error following God, MY understanding of the Word, and yes, therapy! To love God is to trust and obey Him, and not your or the world's understanding (Prov. 3:5-6). It is also to walk in total surrender to His will and way for your life, in full assurance of His ability to cover, sustain, and prosper you in the plan He established for your life before time began. To love yourself is to understand that you are WORTHY and VALUABLE simply because God created you in HIS image and classified you as royalty upon completion. Therefore, you live a lifestyle that aligns itself with that understanding, by holding true to the morals, principles, and values befitting; well —— ROYALTY!

Now, I'm no Confucius, but that is my understanding. And I know that until one has a thorough understanding of their VALUE and WORTH from an internal place, they will ALWAYS be at the mercy of external circumstances and forces that anchor their identity. How do I know that? Well, if your identity is not founded on truths established from an internal place, then it must be founded on external factors. That's why it is possible for a person to project high self-esteem, founded on the things they've accomplished, their talents, what people think or say about them, and what they think or believe about themselves, and STILL not understand why they are WORTHY and valuable absent those external factors.

Back to loving others– a good place to start after having an internal understanding of one's self and a commitment to live a life in alignment with those truths, is to accept your neighbor as they are. That means accepting what or who someone presents themselves to be, at that very moment, as their reality. True acceptance, love, is applied by *not* trying to change them, and without criticism or condemnation.

For example: Let's say you meet someone at a function. Minutes into your conversation, the person begins cursing to the point where every other word is a profanity. Realizing that you, personally, don't subscribe to speaking profanity, view it as a hindrance to your mental well being, and prefer to abstain from using such terms, kindly make your exit and move forward. You don't judge them. You don't criticize or condemn them. And you don't proceed to talk about how XYZ they behave after you walk away. You simply bless them with love as they part, and continue walking your path. If they ask to continue engaging or to connect outside of that venue, you kindly decline, without the need for an explanation, and continue to walk your path. You selflessly "love" them in that way, and as you release them with a blessing, allow for the possibility of encountering a changed version of them one day in the future.

If you resist people with judgment, criticism, or condemnation because of their behavior, or bully them into change, you are not loving them. You are also not loving yourself or upholding your internal standard to reflect the character of God, by accepting them as they are, and simply disengaging uncomplimentary beliefs and behavior with love. God is a God of compassion and forgiveness. He holds no record of offense against us, and to forgive as He forgives means to do the same. Does that mean you stand there and "tolerate" behavior that is contrary to the standard in which you live your life? No. But you do, with compassion, accept that people are who they are until they CHOOSE to become someone else. And until then, they are still loved and valued by God and should be loved by you too – even if it's from a distance ;-).

Prayer for Divine Connections:

Heavenly Father, I thank you that this day starts a new day for me in the journey toward your blessings for my life. I ask Lord that all the connections in my life that are not a part of your plans for me, would be revealed in your name, Jesus. The connections that are evil and toxic that are not there for good but for harm, and that which will hinder me this year, be severed now in Jesus' Name. I pray that all family, friendship, business, and spiritual connection be only the ones that You have for me. Reveal to me by the power of your Holy Spirit, the ones that I need to let go of. Give me grace, courage, and wisdom to follow through with severing these ties, and the words that I will need to speak to these individuals to bring this to a close– if any. I pray that you will open the door for new Divine connections in my business, personal life, ministry, and friendships. I pray your ministering angels are putting everything and everyone in the place where they need to be to fulfill the plans you have for my life. I trust you alone to make these choices for me. You, Father God, who opens doors no one can shut, and closes doors no one can open. I thank You for moving me into Your purpose and blessing for my life. In Jesus Name, and by the power of Your Holy Spirit, Amen!

Practical Application of Loving God

Before we move on to topical scripture verses on love, I want to briefly reflect on the practical application of Loving God; meaning "how" to walk in love toward God.

When I gave my life to Christ at the age of twelve, I was given all kinds of both direct and indirect instruction on how to follow God. Not necessarily "love" Him per se, but how to be a "good Christian," which is what He wants. God, to me, was some faraway being/ruler/judge, waiting to crack me over the head with a spiritual baseball bat at every offense. He was invisible, intangible, and in many ways, an unreal reality in my everyday existence. I know it sounds weird, but that's how I felt.

Fast forward to about three years ago, two years after my divorce following an eighteen-year-old marriage, when I TRULY began seeking God for myself. I wanted to know what it really meant to "love" Him from HIS perspective. I wanted to know how to serve and obey Him from HIS perspective. And I wanted to be sure I was doing it "right."

I'm sure you're just itching to know what happened, or how I obtained such information. Quite simply, the answer is from His Word. Yep, novel, right? It seems so simple, yet most of us don't go straight there after we decide to follow God. Most people usually nosedive into church fellowship and service, learn to emulate the speech and mannerisms of their pastor, leaders, or other seasoned saints, watch popular spiritual teachers for guidance, or come up with what we "feel" should be our new walk. However, God's word is clear, and He promised that His Holy Spirit would lead and guide us into all truth and teach us ALL things. Consulting spiritual leaders and guides for insight is one thing, but even Paul commended the Bereans for going behind him and searching for themselves if those things he taught them were true.

Even in this modern, digital age, we are not absolved of that due diligence. Although we share common experiences, everyone's life, path, and purpose are tailor-made by God for them. You must seek HIM for instruction as to how you should navigate the path He assigned you. You must seek HIM for instruction as to how you, with your unique set of gifts, talents, and abilities, are to love and reverence His presence in your life. There are scripture verses all throughout this book that speak on how we are to walk in love toward God and each other.

I pray you take the time to meditate on them and daily surrender your heart to the Father, asking that He empower you through the Holy Spirit to live out His word. You cannot walk this walk without Him. You cannot love someone you do not know. In your daily prayer time, yes daily, ask the Father to reveal Himself to you. Ask Him to teach you how to live out this Word you are striving to memorize. Ask Him to plant it deep in your heart, and root it way down in your soul. And then open your heart to receive it. Not in the way you want, or you think, or you feel. But in gratitude, and with expectation, open your heart to whatever it is God wants to do in your life. He will make it unequivocally known. He will order your steps and make your path straight. And He will make His love for you clear and evident; to you and all those around you.

Prayer for Deeper Connection and Fellowship with God:

Heavenly Father, I pray that I will be taken into a deeper, more meaningful relationship with You, where I will grow in faith and hear Your still small voice within my soul. Help me to be attentive to Your call and walk-in Your righteousness. I surrender my very being to your will, acknowledging how much I need you, and that I am, and can do NOTHING without You. Open the eyes of my heart. May I see the many blessings you bestow on me, from the greatest to the least. I believe in You, Lord, and thank you for hearing and honoring my request. In Jesus Name, by the power of his Divine and Infinite Spirit, Amen!

Love

Let not steadfast love and faithfulness forsake you; bind them around your neck; write them on the tablet of your heart. So you will find favor and good success in the sight of God and man. Proverbs 3:3-4

Hatred stirs up strife, but love covers all offenses. Proverbs 10:12

A friend loves at all times, and a brother is born for adversity. Proverbs 17:17

Whoever covers an offense seeks love, but he who repeats a matter separates close friends. Proverbs 17:9

But love your enemies, and do good, and lend, expecting nothing in return, and your reward will be great, and you will be sons of the Most High, for he is kind to the ungrateful and the evil. Luke 6:35

"For God so loved the world, that he gave his only Son, that whoever believes in him should not perish but have eternal life." John 3:16

A new commandment I give to you, that you love one another: just as I have loved you, you also are to love one another. By this all people will know that you are my disciples, if you have love for one another. John 13:34-35

"If you love me, you will keep my commandments." John 14:15

Whoever has my commandments and keeps them, he it is who loves me. And he who loves me will be loved by my Father, and I will love him and manifest myself to him. John 14:21

This is my commandment, that you love one another as I have loved you. Greater love has no one than this, that someone lay down his life for his friends. John 15:12-13

Jesus answered, "The most important is, 'Hear, O Israel: The Lord our God, the Lord is one. And you shall love the Lord your God with all your heart and with all your soul and with all your mind and with all your strength.' The second is this: 'You shall love your neighbor as yourself.' There is no other commandment greater than these." Mark 12:29-31

If I speak in the tongues of men and of angels, but have not love, I am a noisy gong or a clanging cymbal. And if I have prophetic powers, and understand all mysteries and all knowledge, and if I have all faith, so as to remove mountains, but have not love, I am nothing. If I give away all I have, and if I deliver up my body to be burned, but have not love, I gain nothing. Love is patient and kind; love does not envy or boast; it is not arrogant or rude. It does not insist on its own way; it is not irritable or resentful; it does not rejoice at wrongdoing, but rejoices with the truth. Love bears all things, believes all things, hopes all things, endures all things. Love never ends. As for prophecies, they will pass away; as for tongues, they will cease; as for knowledge, it will pass away.
1 Corinthians 13:1-8

Let all that you do be done in love. 1 Corinthians 16:14

And above all these put on love, which binds everything together in perfect harmony. Colossians 3:14

But God shows his love for us in that while we were still sinners, Christ died for us. Romans 5:8

Love one another with brotherly affection. Outdo one another in showing honor. Romans 12:10

Owe no one anything, except to love each other, for the one who loves another has fulfilled the law. Romans 13:8

Love does no wrong to a neighbor; therefore love is the fulfilling of the law. Romans 13:10

With all humility and gentleness, with patience, bearing with one another in love, Ephesians 4:2

Above all, keep loving one another earnestly, since love covers a multitude of sins. 1 Peter 4:8

Little children, let us not love in word or talk but in deed and in truth. 1 John 3:18

Beloved, let us love one another, for love is from God, and whoever loves has been born of God and knows God. Anyone who does not love does not know God, because God is love. 1 John 4:7-8

Affirmations for Divine Love

Divine love now dissolves and dissipates every wrong condition in my mind, body, and affairs. Divine love is the most powerful chemical in the universe, and dissolves everything that is not of itself.

All is Divine love. There is nothing but Divine Love.

Because I keep Christ's word, God's love has been perfected in me. This is how I know that I am in Him, that if I say I abide in Him, then I will walk, just like Jesus walked. 1 John 2:5-6

I am beautiful and worthy of love.

I am grateful for the abundance of love in my life

I love all of my brothers and sisters, therefore I abide in God's light, and there is no occasion for stumbling in me. 1 John 2:10

I naturally attract love in my life everywhere I go.

I love everybody and everybody loves me.

I spread love and receive it back many times over.

I love deeply and with passion.

I welcome love with open arms.

My heart is open and ready to love.

I am a richly illuminated child of God, filled with Divine love and wisdom, in which I am guided in all my ways. I am now led into that which is for my highest good.

I love the highest and the best in all people, and I now draw the highest and best people to me for our mutual good and blessing.

There is nothing but God's love and harmony at work here.

Practical Application of Loving our Neighbors

If you love those who love you, what credit is that to you? Even sinners love those who love them. 33 And if you do good to those who are good to you, what credit is that to you? Even sinners do that. 34 And if you lend to those from whom you expect repayment, what credit is that to you? Even sinners lend to sinners, expecting to be repaid in full. 35 But love your enemies, do good to them, and lend to them without expecting to get anything back. Then your reward will be great, and you will be children of the Most High, because he is kind to the ungrateful and wicked. 36 Be merciful, just as your Father is merciful.

Luke 6:32-36 NASB

It is easy to love people who are nice, kind, welcoming, and who you consider to have a "good heart." However, I believe we all can agree that the same cannot be said for those individuals who present as rude, selfish, unkind, abrasive, or any other negative connotation that fits the description. Like any "problem," it would seem like the easiest way to deal with "these people" is to just let them be. Unfortunately, resolving to handle them in any way other than with love (i.e., acceptance) leaves you open to be treated with that same fate.

Yes, you condemn yourself to the same judgment when you criticize your neighbor for their unacceptable behavior, and then banish them with condemnation. I didn't say when you accept them for who they are, and in consideration of your path and the standard by which you live your life, decide if you want to further engage, connect, or continue on your path. I said, judge, criticize, and condemn, which NONE of us is in the position to do. Because the reality is that depending on the lens through which others view life, it is guaranteed that someone will find displeasure in you at some point. Be it right or wrong, just or unjust, one day, someone will have an issue with your looks, attitude, behavior, status, and sometimes quite simply, your presence.

The point is that be it rational or completely unfounded; all believers are called to walk in love toward their neighbors. Not just their Christian brothers and sisters, but also those who don't look, walk, talk, think, and believe as they do. And the reality is that it is not possible to do that with any consistency without the assistance of the Holy Spirit, working in tandem with both a renewed mind and spirit. Salvation takes care of the conversion required to provide us with a new heart/new spirit. However, transformation comes when we renew our mind through God's words, meaning memorizing, speaking, praying, and asking God to show us how to apply the Word of God to our lives on a DAILY BASIS.

The whole purpose of this book is to emphasize the importance of speaking the word of God daily, and when needed, often throughout the day to effectuate lasting transformation in your life. That's why it is laid out the way it is, and I encourage affirming it so often. I've found that as a human being, I am prone to look for comfort, convenience, and safety. I'd rather do something easy before doing something difficult. If there's a less painful or complicated route to take, I'm all in. However, change is not always easy. In fact, sometimes it's downright HARD. And not just for one or two days, or even a week. The process of change can be hard for weeks, and months, and yes, sometimes years.

God help you if you have attachments like people, responsibilities, and an image to maintain, keeping you chained to the very things you are yearning to break free from. So, it's not easy, and when it comes to loving those we deem unlovable or unworthy of our love, we are commanded by God to love them anyway.

So how do you love another person who has proven themselves to be incapable of honoring the Divinity in you and/or reciprocating the love and respect you aspire to give? Well, the word of God gives us clear instruction on how to do this:

"And you shall love the Lord your God with all your heart, and with all your soul, and with all your mind, and with all your strength.' 31 The second is this, 'You shall love your neighbor as yourself.' There is no other commandment greater than these." mark 12:30-31

That said, the next logical question one should have is, how do you love your neighbor as yourself? The best answer I've found to that question in all the years I've lived (forty at this point – to be exact), is to accept them as they are, in respect to who you are and the standard by which you've been called by God to live your life. Now, that sounds easy enough. However, it is not possible if you do not KNOW who you are in God and do not love yourself enough to uphold a righteous standard, regardless of the external influence suggesting otherwise.

I will go into detail about how one can pursue the process of understanding their worth in God, in my reflection on self-worth. But, before you hop over to that section, and I close out this one, I want to share a quick story on a situation God helped me to overcome involving this very topic.

When I accepted my last position with the City of New York, I encountered a person whom EVERYONE deemed impossible to work with. Their behavior wasn't of an overt nature but had a victim spin to it, and was very subtle, yet direct if that makes any sense. This person blocked just about every progressive thing we tried to do, both technologically and administratively. However, I refused to criticize or condemn them. In fact, whenever someone would say something negative to me about this person, I would say, "I love so and so, and they love me," and I meant that. Whenever a conflict would arise with that person, I would say into the atmospheres, "I salute the divinity in you. I see you as God sees you, perfect, made in His image and likeness.

In the meantime, I was also working on getting us assistance from another unit in the agency. Until one day, I encountered a top administrator who casually asked me how things were going, given that I was new. I explained how I was excited to be there but was having difficulty completing key projects due to a lack of assistance and adequate support from this person's unit. This top official listened patiently, before quietly turning to me and saying, "I think I'm going to take this on." I was instructed to put together a report on all that had taken place concerning our productivity issues since my arrival, and within a week, it was delivered.

During that time, there was another team that needed emergency assistance from the difficult employee's unit. It was short notice, and the team in need was unable to follow proper protocols for assistance due to the nature of the emergency. However, this person and their unit refused to accommodate, causing additional issues. All this was taking place in addition to continuing issues in my unit and around the agency. After what I'd been told was over ten years of mayhem and red tape, and four months after I submitted my report, the difficult employee was reassigned and subsequently cleared from my path.

The day word got out, a co-worker walked up to me, cursing the individual, and rejoicing that they would no longer be our headache. But I continued blessing them, offering a prayer that their new location would be a better fit and that they would have peace. I also thanked God for His intervention and for allowing this person to fade harmoniously from my path, as it was not possible to work in harmony.

I did not try to change them; I did not demand that they get in line and do things my way. I accepted them as they were while holding to my standard of showing love and compassion to everyone, regardless of our differences. And I continued to seek God's assistance in bringing harmony by accepting that this was who the person was, that we were not in alignment, disengaging them when possible, and blessing them when not. I also left it up to the Father to either change them so that we could work in harmony, or allow them to harmoniously fade from my path.

Through that experience, God showed me that He would keep His word when we live according to His standard, which is to love Him with all our heart and love our neighbors as ourselves. That situation could have gone so many other ways, had I chosen to handle it MY way. I pray that through continuing to surrender yourself to God's will concerning how to love your neighbors, you'll experience the peace and freedom that comes with accepting people as they are, without criticism or condemnation. That is how God loves you, and truth be told, it doesn't hurt when others love us the same way.

Marriage

Then the Lord God said, "It is not good that the man should be alone; I will make him a helper fit for him." Genesis 2:18

Therefore a man shall leave his father and his mother and hold fast to his wife, and they shall become one flesh. Genesis 2:24

An excellent wife is the crown of her husband, but she who brings shame is like rottenness in his bones. Proverbs 12:4

He who finds a wife finds a good thing and obtains favor from the Lord. Proverbs 18:22

An excellent wife who can find? She is far more precious than jewels. Proverbs 31:10

He answered, "Have you not read that he who created them from the beginning made them male and female, and said, 'Therefore a man shall leave his father and his mother and hold fast to his wife, and the two shall become one flesh'? So they are no longer two but one flesh. What therefore God has joined together, let not man separate." Matthew 19:4-6

Now concerning the things about which you wrote, it is good for a man not to touch a woman. 2 But because of immoralities, each man is to have his own wife, and each woman is to have her own husband. 3 The husband must fulfill his duty to his wife, and likewise also the wife to her husband. 4 The wife does not have authority over her own body, but the husband does; and likewise also the husband does not have authority over his own body, but the wife does. 5 Stop depriving one another, except by agreement for a time, so that you may devote yourselves to prayer, and come together again so that Satan will not tempt you because of your lack of self-control. 1 Corinthians 7:1-5 NASB

But if they cannot exercise self-control, they should marry. For it is better to marry than to burn with passion. 1 Corinthians 7:9

But I want you to understand that the head of every man is Christ, the head of a wife is her husband, and the head of Christ is God. 1 Corinthians 11:3

Do not be unequally yoked with unbelievers. For what partnership has righteousness with lawlessness? Or what fellowship has light with darkness? 2 Corinthians 6:14

And though a man might prevail against one who is alone, two will withstand him—a threefold cord is not quickly broken. Ecclesiastes 4:12

Wives, be subject to your own husbands, as to the Lord. 23 For the husband is the head of the wife, as Christ also is the head of the church, He Himself being the Savior of the body. 24 But as the church is subject to Christ, so also the wives ought to be to their husbands in everything.
25 Husbands, love your wives, just as Christ also loved the church and gave Himself up for her, 26 so that He might sanctify her, having cleansed her by the washing of water with the word, 27 that He might present to Himself the church in all her glory, having no spot or wrinkle or any such thing; but that she would be holy and blameless. 28 So husbands ought also to love their own wives as their own bodies. He who loves his own wife loves himself; 29 for no one ever hated his own flesh but nourishes and cherishes it, just as Christ also does the church
Ephesians 5:22-29 NASB

However, let each one of you love his wife as himself, and let the wife see that she respects her husband. Ephesians 5:33

Wives, submit to your husbands, as is fitting in the Lord. Husbands, love your wives and do not be harsh with them. Colossians 3:18-19

Let marriage be held in honor among all, and let the marriage bed be undefiled, for God will judge the sexually immoral and adulterous.
Hebrews 13:4

Likewise, husbands, live with your wives in an understanding way, showing honor to the woman as the weaker vessel, since they are heirs with you of the grace of life, so that your prayers may not be hindered. 1 Peter 3:7

Affirmations for Divine Marriage Commitment

Father– I give thanks for a Divine right selection, a marriage partner after your heart. Someone who loves You and honors You in all their ways. It breaks their heart to break your heart, and they love me unconditionally. I thank you that they accept and love me as I am, as I do them. Their heart is open, available, and ready for a marriage commitment. They are capable of love, desire to love someone in a marriage commitment and love everyone attached to me, as I love them the same.

I draw love and romance into my life with ease.

I am attracting a Divine right selection, ready to compliment me, just as they are.

I am the Divine right selection I desire to attract, in God's perfect time.

Patience – Perseverance

Be still before the Lord and wait patiently for him; fret not yourself over the one who prospers in his way, over the man who carries out evil devices! Refrain from anger, and forsake wrath! Fret not yourself; it tends only to evil. For the evildoers shall be cut off, but those who wait for the Lord shall inherit the land. Psalm 37:7-9

To the choirmaster. A Psalm of David. I waited patiently for the Lord; he inclined to me and heard my cry. Psalm 40:1

115

With patience, a ruler may be persuaded, and a soft tongue will break a bone. Proverbs 25:15

Better is the end of a thing than its beginning, and the patient in spirit is better than the proud in spirit. Ecclesiastes 7:8

But they who wait for the Lord shall renew their strength; they shall mount up with wings like eagles; they shall run and not be weary; they shall walk and not faint. Isaiah 40:31

But if we hope for what we do not see, we wait for it with patience. Romans 8:25

And let us not grow weary of doing good, for in due season we will reap, if we do not give up. Galatians 6:9

And we urge you, brothers, admonish the idle, encourage the fainthearted, help the weak, be patient with them all. 1 Thessalonians 5:14

May you be strengthened with all power, according to his glorious might, for all endurance and patience with joy, Colossians 1:11

For you have need of endurance, so that when you have done the will of God, you may receive what is promised. Hebrews 10:36

Be patient, therefore, brothers, until the coming of the Lord. See how the farmer waits for the precious fruit of the earth, being patient about it until it receives the early and the late rains. You also be patient. Establish your hearts, for the coming of the Lord is at hand. James 5:7-8

For this is a gracious thing, when, mindful of God, one endures sorrows while suffering unjustly. For what credit is it if, when you sin and are beaten for it, you endure? But if when you do good and suffer for it, you endure, this is a gracious thing in the sight of God. For to this, you have been called, because Christ also suffered for you, leaving you an example, so that you might follow in his steps. He committed no sin, neither was deceit found in his mouth. When he was reviled, he did not revile in return; when he suffered, he did not threaten, but continued entrusting himself to him who judges justly. 1 Peter 2:19-23

Peace

Great peace have those who love your law; nothing can make them stumble. Psalm 119:165

When a man's ways please the Lord, he makes even his enemies to be at peace with him. Proverbs 16:7

You keep him in perfect peace whose mind is stayed on you, because he trusts in you. Isaiah 26:3

I have said these things to you, that in me you may have peace. In the world you will have tribulation. But take heart; I have overcome the world. John 16:33

For to set the mind on the flesh is death, but to set the mind on the Spirit is life and peace. Romans 8:6

So then let us pursue what makes for peace and for mutual upbuilding. Romans 14:19

May the God of hope fill you with all joy and peace in believing, so that by the power of the Holy Spirit you may abound in hope. Romans 15:13

If possible, so far as it depends on you, live peaceably with all. Romans 12:18

But because of the temptation to sexual immorality, each man should have his own wife and each woman her own husband. 1 Corinthians 7:2

For God is not a God of confusion but of peace. As in all the churches of the saints, 1 Corinthians 14:33

Finally, brothers, rejoice. Aim for restoration, comfort one another, agree with one another, live in peace; and the God of love and peace will be with you. 2 Corinthians 13:11

Be anxious for nothing, but in everything by prayer and supplication with thanksgiving let your requests be made known to God. 7 And the peace of God, which surpasses all comprehension, will guard your hearts and your minds in Christ Jesus. 8 Finally, brethren, whatever is true, whatever is honorable, whatever is right, whatever is pure, whatever is lovely, whatever is of good repute, if there is any excellence and if anything worthy of praise, dwell on these things. 9 The things you have learned and received and heard and seen in me, practice these things, and the God of peace will be with you. Philippians 4:6-9 NASB

Now may the Lord of peace himself give you peace at all times in every way. The Lord be with you all. 2 Thessalonians 3:16

Strive for peace with everyone, and for the holiness without which no one will see the Lord. Hebrews 12:14

And a harvest of righteousness is sown in peace by those who make peace. James 3:18

Let him turn away from evil and do good; let him seek peace and pursue it. 1 Peter 3:11

Poverty

For there will never cease to be poor in the land. Therefore I command you, 'You shall open wide your hand to your brother, to the needy and to the poor, in your land.' Deuteronomy 15:11

He raises up the poor from the dust; he lifts the needy from the ash heap to make them sit with princes and inherit a seat of honor. For the pillars of the earth are the Lord's, and on them he has set the world.
1 Samuel 2:8

I have been young, and now am old, yet I have not seen the righteous forsaken or his children begging for bread. Psalm 37:25

I know that the Lord will maintain the cause of the afflicted, and will execute justice for the needy. Psalm 140:12

Better is a little with the fear of the Lord than great treasure and trouble with it. Proverbs 15:16

Love not sleep, lest you come to poverty; open your eyes, and you will have plenty of bread. Proverbs 20:13

The plans of the diligent lead surely to abundance, but everyone who is hasty comes only to poverty. Proverbs 21:5

The rich rules over the poor, and the borrower is the slave of the lender. Proverbs 22:7

When the poor and needy seek water, and there is none, and their tongue is parched with thirst, I the Lord will answer them; I the God of Israel will not forsake them. Isaiah 41:17

But if anyone has the world's goods and sees his brother in need, yet closes his heart against him, how does God's love abide in him?
1 John 3:17

Prayer

If my people who are called by my name humble themselves, and pray and seek my face and turn from their wicked ways, then I will hear from heaven and will forgive their sin and heal their land. 2 Chronicles 7:14

When the righteous cry for help, the Lord hears and delivers them out of all their troubles. Psalm 34:17

The rich rules over the poor, and the borrower is the slave of the lender. Proverbs 22:7

A little sleep, a little slumber, a little folding of the hands to rest, and poverty will come upon you like a robber, and want like an armed man. Proverbs 24:33-34

Call to me and I will answer you, and will tell you great and hidden things that you have not known. Jeremiah 33:3

And when you pray, you must not be like the hypocrites. For they love to stand and pray in the synagogues and at the street corners, that they may be seen by others. Truly, I say to you, they have received their reward. But when you pray, go into your room and shut the door and pray to your Father who is in secret. And your Father who sees in secret will reward you. And when you pray, do not heap up empty phrases as the Gentiles do, for they think that they will be heard for their many words. Do not be like them, for your Father knows what you need before you ask him. Matthew 6:5-8

But I say to you who hear, Love your enemies, do good to those who hate you, bless those who curse you, pray for those who abuse you. Luke 6:27-28

And he told them a parable to the effect that they ought always to pray and not lose heart. Luke 18:1

Therefore I tell you, whatever you ask in prayer, believe that you have received it, and it will be yours. Mark 11:24

Praying at all times in the Spirit, with all prayer and supplication. To that end keep alert with all perseverance, making supplication for all the saints, Ephesians 6:18

Do not be anxious about anything, but in everything by prayer and supplication with thanksgiving let your requests be made known to God. Philippians 4:6

Continue steadfastly in prayer, being watchful in it with thanksgiving. Colossians 4:2

Pray without ceasing . . . 1 Thessalonians 5:17

First of all, then, I urge that supplications, prayers, intercessions, and thanksgivings be made for all people, for kings and all who are in high positions, that we may lead a peaceful and quiet life, godly and dignified in every way. This is good, and it is pleasing in the sight of God our Savior, who desires all people to be saved and to come to the knowledge of the truth. 1 Timothy 2:1-4

I desire then that in every place the men should pray, lifting holy hands without anger or quarreling; 1 Timothy 2:8

Therefore, confess your sins to one another and pray for one another, that you may be healed. The prayer of a righteous person has great power as it is working. James 5:16

Pride

The fear of the Lord is hatred of evil. Pride and arrogance and the way of evil and perverted speech I hate. Proverbs 8:13

When pride comes, then comes disgrace, but with the humble is wisdom. Proverbs 11:2

Pride goes before destruction, and a haughty spirit before a fall. Proverbs 16:18

Let another praise you, and not your own mouth; a stranger, and not your own lips. Proverbs 27:2

One's pride will bring him low, but he who is lowly in spirit will obtain honor. Proverbs 29:23

Better is the end of a thing than its beginning, and the patient in spirit is better than the proud in spirit. Ecclesiastes 7:8

For by the grace given to me I say to everyone among you not to think of himself more highly than he ought to think, but to think with sober judgment, each according to the measure of faith that God has assigned. Romans 12:3

Live in harmony with one another. Do not be haughty, but associate with the lowly. Never be wise in your own sight. Romans 12:16

"Let the one who boasts, boast in the Lord." For it is not the one who commends himself who is approved, but the one whom the Lord commends. 2 Corinthians 10:17-18

For if anyone thinks he is something, when he is nothing, he deceives himself. Galatians 6:3

Humble yourselves before the Lord, and he will exalt you. James 4:10

Do nothing from rivalry or conceit, but in humility count others more significant than yourselves. Philippians 2:3

Likewise, you who are younger, be subject to the elders. Clothe yourselves, all of you, with humility toward one another, for "God opposes the proud but gives grace to the humble." 1 Peter 5:5

Prosperity

This Book of the Law shall not depart from your mouth, but you shall meditate on it day and night, so that you may be careful to do according to all that is written in it. For then you will make your way prosperous, and then you will have good success. Joahua1:8

How blessed is the man who does not walk in the counsel of the wicked, Nor stand in the path of sinners, Nor sit in the seat of scoffers!2 But his delight is in the law of the Lord, And in His law, he meditates day and night.3 He will be like a tree firmly planted by streams of water, Which yields its fruit in its season And its leaf does not wither; And in whatever he does, he prospers. Psalm 1:1-3 NASB

Oh, taste and see that the Lord is good! Blessed is the man who takes refuge in him! Oh, fear the Lord, you his saints, for those who fear him have no lack! The young lions suffer want and hunger, but those who seek the Lord lack no good thing. Psalm 34:8-10

For the Lord God is a sun and shield; the Lord bestows favor and honor. No good thing does he withhold from those who walk uprightly. Psalm 84:11

Praise the Lord! Blessed is the man who fears the Lord, who greatly delights in his commandments! His offspring will be mighty in the land; the generation of the upright will be blessed. Wealth and riches are in his house, and his righteousness endures forever. Psalm 112:1-3

You shall eat the fruit of the labor of your hands; you shall be blessed, and it shall be well with you. Psalm 128:2

The blessing of the Lord makes rich, and he adds no sorrow with it. Proverbs 10:22

In the day of prosperity be joyful, and in the day of adversity consider: God has made the one as well as the other, so that man may not find out anything that will be after him. Ecclesiastes 7:14

"I the Lord search the heart and test the mind, to give every man according to his ways, according to the fruit of his deeds." Jeremiah 17:10

And God is able to make all grace abound to you, so that having all sufficiency in all things at all times, you may abound in every good work. 2 Corinthians 9:8

And my God will supply every need of yours according to his riches in glory in Christ Jesus. Philippians 4:19

Protection

The Lord will fight for you, and you have only to be silent. Exodus 14:14

But you, O Lord, are a shield about me, my glory, and the lifter of my head. Psalm 3:3

The angel of the Lord encamps around those who fear him, and delivers them. Psalm 34:7

It is better to take refuge in the Lord than to trust in man. Psalm 118:8

Though I walk in the midst of trouble, you preserve my life; you stretch out your hand against the wrath of my enemies, and your right hand delivers me. Psalm 138:7

The name of the Lord is a strong tower; the righteous man runs into it and is safe. Proverbs 18:10

Every word of God proves true; he is a shield to those who take refuge in him. Proverbs 30:5

No weapon that is formed against you will prosper; And every tongue that accuses you in judgment you will condemn. This is the heritage of the servants of the Lord, And their vindication is from Me, declares the Lord. Isaiah 54:17 NASB

The Lord is good, a stronghold in the day of trouble; he knows those who take refuge in him. Nahum 1:7

What then shall we say to these things? If God is for us, who can be against us? Romans 8:31

But the Lord is faithful. He will establish you and guard you against the evil one. 2 Thessalonians 3:3

Righteousness

The eyes of the Lord are toward the righteous and his ears toward their cry. Psalm 34:15

Blessed are they who observe justice, who do righteousness at all times! Psalm 106:3

The righteousness of the blameless keeps his way straight, but the wicked falls by his own wickedness. Proverbs 11:5

To do righteousness and justice is more acceptable to the Lord than sacrifice. Proverbs 21:3

Sow for yourselves righteousness; reap steadfast love; break up your fallow ground, for it is the time to seek the Lord, that he may come and rain righteousness upon you. Hosea 10:12

For what does the Scripture say? "Abraham believed God, and it was credited to him as righteousness." 4 Now to the one who works, his wage is not credited as a favor, but as what is due. 5 But to the one who does not work, but believes in Him who justifies the ungodly, his faith is credited as righteousness. Romans 4:3-5 NASB

For if, because of one man's trespass, death reigned through that one man, much more will those who receive the abundance of grace and the free gift of righteousness reign in life through the one man Jesus Christ. Romans 5:17

In order that the righteous requirement of the law might be fulfilled in us, who walk not according to the flesh but according to the Spirit. For those who live according to the flesh set their minds on the things of the flesh, but those who live according to the Spirit set their minds on the things of the Spirit. For to set the mind on the flesh is death, but to set the mind on the Spirit is life and peace. Romans 8:4-6

For our sake he made him to be sin who knew no sin, so that in him we might become the righteousness of God. 2 Corinthians 5:21

So flee youthful passions and pursue righteousness, faith, love, and peace, along with those who call on the Lord from a pure heart.
2 Timothy 2:22

For the eyes of the Lord are on the righteous, and his ears are open to their prayer. But the face of the Lord is against those who do evil.
1 Peter 3:12

We know that everyone who has been born of God does not keep on sinning, but he who was born of God protects him, and the evil one does not touch him. 1 John 5:18

Salvation

Jesus answered him, "Truly, truly, I say to you, unless one is born again he cannot see the kingdom of God." John 3:3

Truly, truly, I say to you, whoever hears my word and believes him who sent me has eternal life. He does not come into judgment, but has passed from death to life. John 5:24

For God so loved the world, that he gave his only Son, that whoever believes in him should not perish but have eternal life. For God did not send his Son into the world to condemn the world, but in order that the world might be saved through him. Whoever believes in him is not condemned, but whoever does not believe is condemned already, because he has not believed in the name of the only Son of God. John 3:16-18

Whoever believes in the Son has eternal life; whoever does not obey the Son shall not see life, but the wrath of God remains on him. John 3:36

"And there is salvation in no one else, for there is no other name under heaven given among men by which we must be saved." Acts 4:12

Then he brought them out and said, "Sirs, what must I do to be saved?" And they said, "Believe in the Lord Jesus, and you will be saved, you and your household." And they spoke the word of the Lord to him and to all who were in his house. And he took them the same hour of the night and washed their wounds; and he was baptized at once, he and all his family. Acts 16:30-33

But God shows his love for us in that while we were still sinners, Christ died for us. Romans 5:8

Because if you confess with your mouth that Jesus is Lord and believe in your heart that God raised him from the dead, you will be saved. For with the heart, one believes and is justified, and with the mouth, one confesses and is saved. Romans 10:9-10

For by grace, you have been saved through faith. And this is not your own doing; it is the gift of God, not a result of works, so that no one may boast. Ephesians 2:8-9

Although this book was made to be a practical resource for converted believers, who have already accepted Jesus Christ and are now seeking to be transformed by renewing their mind through God's word, you never know whose hands God's word may fall into. Therefore, I've included the Steps to Salvation, not just for believers who want to know how to lead someone to Christ, but also for someone who has not yet accepted Christ, and is feeling led to do so after discovering this book. The Steps to Salvation are quite simple, and most importantly, require a heart open and ready to be brought back into fellowship with God.

Three Steps to Salvation: A B Cs

A quick web search on the "Steps to Salvation," will turn up anywhere from three to, in one case, TWELVE steps to salvation. However, I've listed three, which tie repentance of sin and asking for forgiveness into the first step, since that is a part of admitting you are a sinner.

1) **Admit:** To God and yourself that you are a sinner, by repenting of your sins, and asking God for His forgiveness. Romans 3:10, 23, Acts 3:19

2) **Believe:** The Good News – Jesus died for your sins, rose from the dead, and is returning for all who believe in Him. John 3:16, John 15:15, Romans 5:8

3) **Confess:** That Jesus is Lord. Romans 10:9-10

Prayer of Salvation

Jesus, I know that I am a sinner in need of a savior. I ask You to forgive me of my sins. I believe that You died on the cross to save me from my sins. I now ask You to be Lord of my life, and I promise to commit my life to You. Amen!

Sin (Consequences – Repentance – Forgiveness)

Create in me a clean heart, O God, and renew a right spirit within me. Psalm 51:10

Whoever conceals his transgressions will not prosper, but he who confesses and forsakes them will obtain mercy. Proverbs 28:13

But your iniquities have made a separation between you and your God, and your sins have hidden his face from you so that he does not hear. Isaiah 59:2

And he said, "What comes out of a person is what defiles him. For from within, out of the heart of man, come evil thoughts, sexual immorality, theft, murder, adultery, coveting, wickedness, deceit, sensuality, envy, slander, pride, foolishness. All these evil things come from within, and they defile a person." Mark 7:20-23

Therefore God gave them up in the lusts of their hearts to impurity, to the dishonoring of their bodies among themselves, because they exchanged the truth about God for a lie and worshiped and served the creature rather than the Creator, who is blessed forever! Amen. Romans 1:24-25

For the wages of sin is death, but the free gift of God is eternal life in Christ Jesus our Lord. Romans 6:23

Or do you not know that your body is a temple of the Holy Spirit within you, whom you have from God? You are not your own, for you were bought with a price. So glorify God in your body. 1 Corinthians 6:19-20

Now the works of the flesh are evident: sexual immorality, impurity, sensuality, idolatry, sorcery, enmity, strife, jealousy, fits of anger, rivalries, dissensions, divisions, envy, drunkenness, orgies, and things like these. I warn you, as I warned you before, that those who do such things will not inherit the kingdom of God. Galatians 5:19-21

For if we go on sinning deliberately after receiving the knowledge of the truth, there no longer remains a sacrifice for sins, Hebrews 10:26

Then desire when it has conceived gives birth to sin, and sin when it is fully grown brings forth death. James 1:5

So whoever knows the right thing to do and fails to do it, for him it is sin. James 4:17

If we say we have no sin, we deceive ourselves, and the truth is not in us. If we confess our sins, he is faithful and just to forgive us our sins and to cleanse us from all unrighteousness. If we say we have not sinned, we make him a liar, and his word is not in us. 1 John 1:8-10

Everyone who makes a practice of sinning also practices lawlessness; sin is lawlessness. 1 John 3:4

Speaking

Set a guard, O Lord, over my mouth; keep watch over the door of my lips! Psalm 141:3

Whoever guards his mouth preserves his life; he who opens wide his lips comes to ruin. Proverbs 13:3

A soft answer turns away wrath, but a harsh word stirs up anger. Proverbs 15:1

The heart of the righteous ponders how to answer, but the mouth of the wicked pours out evil things. Proverbs 15:28

Even a fool who keeps silent is considered wise; when he closes his lips, he is deemed intelligent. Proverbs 17:28

A word fitly spoken is like apples of gold in a setting of silver. Proverbs 25:11

A fool gives full vent to his spirit, but a wise man quietly holds it back. Proverbs 29:11

"For by your words, you will be justified, and by your words, you will be condemned." Matthew 12:37

Let no corrupting talk come out of your mouths, but only such as is good for building up, as fits the occasion, that it may give grace to those who hear. Ephesians 4:29

Let there be no filthiness nor foolish talk nor crude joking, which are out of place, but instead let there be thanksgiving. Ephesians 5:4

Let your speech always be gracious, seasoned with salt, so that you may know how you ought to answer each person. Colossians 4:6

To speak evil of no one, to avoid quarreling, to be gentle, and to show perfect courtesy toward all people. Titus 3:2

Know this, my beloved brothers: let every person be quick to hear, slow to speak, slow to anger; James 1:19

But no human being can tame the tongue. It is a restless evil, full of deadly poison. With it, we bless our Lord and Father, and with it, we curse people who are made in the likeness of God. From the same mouth come blessing and cursing. My brothers, these things ought not to be so. James 3:8-10

Do not repay evil for evil or reviling for reviling, but on the contrary, bless, for to this you were called, that you may obtain a blessing.
1 Peter 3:9

Spiritual Warfare – Whole Armor of God

The Lord will cause your enemies who rise against you to be defeated before you. They shall come out against you one way and flee before you seven ways. Deuteronomy 28:7

For though we walk in the flesh, we are not waging war according to the flesh. For the weapons of our warfare are not of the flesh but have Divine power to destroy strongholds. We destroy arguments and every lofty opinion raised against the knowledge of God, and take every thought captive to obey Christ . . . 2 Corinthians 10:3-5

For we do not wrestle against flesh and blood, but against the rulers, against the authorities, against the cosmic powers over this present darkness, against the spiritual forces of evil in the heavenly places.
Ephesians 6:12

Submit yourselves therefore to God. Resist the devil, and he will flee from you. James 4:7

Be sober-minded; be watchful. Your adversary, the devil, prowls around like a roaring lion, seeking someone to devour. Resist him, firm in your faith, knowing that the same kinds of suffering are being experienced by your brotherhood throughout the world. 1 Peter 5:8-9

But the Lord is faithful. He will establish you and guard you against the evil one. 2 Thessalonians 3:3

The Whole Armor of God

The word of God provides believers with the necessary tools required to STAND against the enemy as GOD fights our battles. However, based on how most of us "fight," one looking on from the side would think that this armor is just for show, and only useful when we've done all we could do and now need to call on God for assistance. That is not how it should be used. In fact, each one of us should start our day by dressing ourselves in the equipment provided, by acknowledging our need for God to war against the enemy as we protect our mind, heart, and assignment with His Divine armor.

God's word outlines our armor as follows:

Therefore, take up the full armor of God, so that you will be able to resist in the evil day, and having done everything, to stand firm. 14 Stand firm, therefore, having girded your loins with truth, and having put on the breastplate of righteousness, 15 and having shod your feet with the preparation of the gospel of peace; 16 in addition to all, taking up the shield of faith with which you will be able to extinguish all the flaming arrows of the evil one. 17 And take the helmet of salvation, and the sword of the Spirit, which is the word of God.18 With all prayer and petition pray at all times in the Spirit, and with this in view, be on the alert with all perseverance and petition for all the saints. Ephesians 6:13-18 NASB

So, how do we dress in God's royal armor? Through praying on our armor, and then endeavoring to activate each piece through speaking and applying God's word in every situation, per His leading. As with anything we desire to last in our lives, we must first acknowledge that desire through our spoken commitment. We then carry out that commitment with consistent action. As you've probably already realized, you CANNOT live the life of a believer alone. You NEED God's help. Starting your day with prayer, acknowledging the armor our Father has provided, and activating it through the practice of affirming God's word, is required in order for your armor to be most effective at quenching the fiery darts of the enemy.

Remember: the enemy can't put his hands on you. It's important to reiterate that you are not being commanded to fight. Just to take up the Whole Armor of God that He provided to help you STAND and resist the enemy until he flees. And he will flee, because God's word promised he would when you resist him. Don't ask him questions. Don't curse him out. Don't even rebuke him. Simply resist him with God's armor, which you will not be able to do if you are not properly dressed.

Here's a prayer you can add to your morning prayers before you start your day. Hopefully, you are starting your day with a bit more than, "Bless me, Lord, in this day. Help me not to go off on anybody. Help me to get to work safely and return back home again safe. In Jesus name, Amen." Hopefully, you are connecting with your heavenly Father with a bit more than that. But even if you're only able to muster three words each morning, "Thank you, Lord," I encourage you to add this short prayer to your script. I believe it was adapted from a prayer drafted by God's Spoken Word Ministries. However, I could only find portions on their site when I did a full search a few months ago. I first found this prayer online last year and added my own emphasis, which has made the original hard to find. Therefore, I encourage you to edit and enhance it to your liking, for your good and God's glory.

Whole Armor of God Prayer

Father God, thank You for your Armor, which You have given to me to fight against the enemy. I know that my war is not against flesh and blood; therefore, I stand firm with the belt of truth buckled around my waist; thank you for your word. Your word is truth, and I pray that every decision that I make today would be based on your word. I put the breastplate of righteousness in place to protect my heart for out of the heart the mouth speaks. May the words of my mouth and the meditation of my heart be acceptable in your sight, Oh Lord, my Rock, and my Redeemer, and with my feet fitted with the readiness that comes from the gospel of peace. In addition to all this, I take up the shield of faith with which I can extinguish all the flaming arrows of the evil one. I believe your word, and I have faith in it. Taking the helmet of salvation to protect my mind, my thoughts, my dreams, my vision, and what I see. Thank you for saving me. And the sword of the Spirit, which is the word of God, gives me the scriptures that I need to speak against the enemy when he comes to attack me, in Jesus' Name, and by the power of Your Holy Spirit. Amen.

Strength

Be strong and courageous. Do not fear or be in dread of them, for it is the Lord your God who goes with you. He will not leave you or forsake you. Deuteronomy 31:6

Have I not commanded you? Be strong and courageous. Do not be frightened, and do not be dismayed, for the Lord your God is with you wherever you go. Joshua 1:9

The Lord is my strength and my shield; in him my heart trusts, and I am helped; my heart exults, and with my song I give thanks to him. The Lord is the strength of his people; he is the saving refuge of his anointed. Psalm 28:7-8

Be strong, and let your heart take courage, all you who wait for the Lord! Psalm 31:24

My flesh and my heart may fail, but God is the strength of my heart and my portion forever. Psalm 73:26

He gives power to the faint, and to him who has no might he increases strength. Isaiah 40:29

But they who wait for the Lord shall renew their strength; they shall mount up with wings like eagles; they shall run and not be weary; they shall walk and not faint. Isaiah 40:31

But he said to me, "My grace is sufficient for you, for my power is made perfect in weakness." Therefore I will boast all the more gladly of my weaknesses, so that the power of Christ may rest upon me. For the sake of Christ, then, I am content with weaknesses, insults, hardships, persecutions, and calamities. For when I am weak, then I am strong. 2 Corinthians 12:9-1

Reflections on Divine Surrender

Then Jesus told his disciples, "If anyone would come after me, let him deny himself and take up his cross and follow me. 25 For whoever would save his life will lose it, but whoever loses his life for my sake will find it. 26 For what will it profit a man if he gains the whole world and forfeits his soul? Or what shall a man give in return for his soul?"
Matthew 16:24-26 NASB

This reflection was my last and hardest to write. I delayed for some time because there are so many angles in which to approach the topic. However, the one I will be pursuing is founded in my belief that one cannot even begin to come into the knowledge of their self-worth in God until they first decide to surrender themselves to HIS process.

So, I begin with this question: How do you KNOW that the person you are is the highest expression of yourself AND that the purpose you are walking in was unequivocally laid by God, if you have not undergone the process of laying yourself and your plans on His altar for searching? I mean, if you have never laid yourself before God, and said, "Father, here's who I believe myself to be, is this the image you have of me? Or, "Father, here is what I believe I am supposed to do, is this the plan you have for me?" and WAIT for Him to make His answer plain; how do you KNOW that the person you present to this world, and the path in which you are currently traveling, were formed in Divine mind, and not your own?

The truth is that there aren't too many people (including believers) that can say that, because we as a society are socially conditioned to pick an ideal image and aspire to be it in order to receive acceptance and validation. Most of us were not raised to seek out the approval and validation of God and God alone. I know I wasn't, and as a result, I too picked out an acceptable image that projected a strong, Godly, independent, and successful woman (i.e., the right clothes, hair, disposition, etc.), with a noteworthy and esteemed career to match, in efforts to affirm my value and worth in this world. I married someone who had the "potential" to be everything I had in my head (no one's perfect, right?), and I intended to push him and myself to produce and maintain the status and lifestyle that would solidify our position and value in this earth.

I had no idea that going to God and asking Him to search me and reveal my Divine identity was even a thing. I didn't know anything about Divine self-worth and that my value was automatically assigned to me when God created me. I always thought that I had to decide who I would be and where I was going, based on what *I* wanted. And that is true to some extent. However, until one goes before the Father to learn of their Divine identity and subsequent purpose in Him, the "person" they present to the world will be a construct of their own imagination, and everything "it" produces will be subject to its limitations, and thus, unsustainable.

In our opening scripture verse, God's word says that whoever seeks to save their life will lose it. Well, let's think about that for a bit. How many of you have spent a number of years, and maybe even a lifetime trying to figure out how to look, how to act, who to marry, where to work, and how not to lose your mind managing all the decisions YOU made, trying to answer those questions and build some kind of LIFE? Not to mention the pressure from family and friends who want to be sure that YOUR choices amount to something, or provide for them, or make them look good, or all of the above and more.

The verse then goes on to say that he who loses his life for the cause of Christ will find it. So, if we give up our time, talent, and treasure for the things of God (per His direct and unequivocal leading, not brow-beating from the pastor, or anyone else), we will find our life. And that sounds admirable, although it doesn't say how one should give up their life, or make the distinction between following God and being taken advantage of by the "church." Which then leads to the final part of that verse, which questions thus: "What does it profit a man to gain the whole world and lose his soul?" And that statement, I believe, is key to solving this equation, because it begs the question, how does one "lose their soul" while pursuing their own life?

Since I didn't conduct a nationwide poll of the world's top spiritual minds, I decided to use myself as an example. As I mentioned in the introduction, I accepted Christ at age twelve. I then made what I believe was every effort to follow God the way I knew best. After first attempting to follow Him straight from the bible and being condemned for trying to be "perfect," I decided to do what I saw most people do by making my own plans and asking God to bless them. It didn't help that all of my decisions were steeped in a foundation of fear and selfishness, as my motivation was self-protection and self-validation. I did not intentionally set out to walk this way, but it was what I saw, and it seemed like the way things should be.

I then married someone while I was very young, seeking to further secure my life with someone who was also saved, and who seemed nice, stable, and able to partner with me in this life. Mind you, I did ask God about him (meaning other people), but there were no lightning strikes, and he looked like a good fit to my plan, we survived thirteen weeks of pre-marital counseling, so I went with it. My decision to marry him was not about accepting him as he was and loving him unconditionally, as I wasn't even doing that for myself. I also had no real intention of submitting to him or respecting him as the leader of our home, evidenced by the fact that I hyphenated my last name when we married – and that was intentional. That was also the first time I sold my soul, but I didn't know it.

I then began to look at other successful women and how they presented themselves; smart, independent, strong, and "unbossed," and decided I would be that way too. It was a subconscious decision that I felt was harmless, and that would provide me with an ultimate sense of security concerning my personal relationships. Operating this way, I would not be taken advantage of, and I would always maintain control. That was the second time I sold my soul, because operating that way robbed me of intimate connections and the joy of truly learning to walk in love toward others. But that was just the beginning.

The last area of soul exploitation came in regard to my career path. I had always been in the creative field, starting from junior high, which was a performing arts school. I picked the easiest, non-public major there, which was art. I continued on that path all the way through college, while simultaneously serving in ministry. As I was now grown, and realizing that adulthood wasn't all I'd imagined, I figured I'd throw myself into ministry, in hopes that I would be guaranteed a successful life if I did EVERYTHING God asked me. And I do mean everything. I neglected my marriage and myself for years. I had no concept of who I was, why I was working in the field I was, and why I was serving so hard in the ministry. I just felt like I "had" to, if I wanted to be blessed and safe. And so, I continued selling my soul, even in what I thought was in service to God in order to save myself. The series of decisions that led me along that path led to destruction in some areas (my marriage), unfulfillment in others (my career), and a lack of genuine connection in my relationships (family, friends, acquaintances, etc.), because I wasn't connected to "me".

It wasn't until that "situationship" I spoke of earlier happened that I began to see what was taking place. And not because I was voluntarily trying to change, but because the situation had become so intolerable that I needed to make a change that would never bring me back to that place. It was during that time that I finally went before God and asked him to search my heart. I asked Him to tear down the person I'd constructed if it wasn't His Divine plan, and open my eyes to the person HE called me to be. I asked Him to order my steps and make my path straight and remove anything and anyone from my life who was not in His Divine plan for me. That included new male "friends," my associations, my plans, and yes, even my career.

Within a matter of two years, I not only looked completely different, but God somehow orchestrated everything in a way that caused everyone I was associated with to completely dissolve from my life. I was learning to walk in obedience to God and was changing; no longer having any of the attachments I'd known prior. However, there was the matter of my career I was waiting for confirmation on. And it was during this time that God began to place a vision in my heart to not only be a wife again (this time, His way) but also a stay-at-home mother, no longer working a nine-to-five. I could not understand where that vision was coming from. But it felt like it was the way it should have been from the beginning. I also began to see myself with a different hairstyle and no longer wearing the business attire I wore every day.

It was totally unreal until the Covid-19 pandemic hit, and everything stopped. The month prior, I'd just told God that the only way I could just up and stop my career was if He stopped it. Now, here we are in the middle of a pandemic, and everything did indeed stop. I'm not saying that my prayer caused the pandemic. LOL! I believe that a lot of people were in my position concerning a number of things, requiring a worldwide "PAUSE." Notwithstanding, I used that time to allow God to really make clear the desires I believe He'd given me, surrendering myself to His leading.

I'm happy to report that just a mere few months after that yielding, through a series of God-ordained events, I am transitioning from the nine-to-five career to that stay-at-home mom. I am not yet a wife (in the visible realm) as God is still shifting some things so that His Divine right selection will present in His perfect time. However, I did have one person reach out to me stating that he had changed, and he was the one (he was not), indicating that God's choice is close, being that an incomplete manifestation (sign) of His promise had presented.

This being one of my last reflections in this book, I want to impress upon you the importance, and really the requirement of placing yourself before the Father to understand His blueprint concerning all things YOU, before you take another step in life. If it turns out that you are completely off course and that everything must be blown to bits in order to set things straight, it's better that happens sooner than later. God promised to work everything for your good, which includes the consequences of selfish decisions made in pursuit of your own self-interest. Your issue may not be self-protection, but just knowing who you are in Christ and being validated in that. Issues with self-worth can cause people to attempt being all things to all people in search of validation. This makes it impossible for them to hold on to one standard of living, as they have none. It may be numbing yourself with drugs and alcohol so that you don't have to face your past, your current way of life, or your feelings of inadequacy due to both. Whatever it is, until you place yourself before God for His take, you will always be guessing, proving, and striving to be someone and do something He may not have called you to be and do.

Believe it or not, and for a myriad of reasons, there are doctors, lawyers, teachers, drug dealers, and even preachers (yes preachers), who sell their souls to practice noble and/or lucrative professions, in full ignorance or dismissal to who they were called by God to be. And regardless of the vocation, just like with sin, there is no variation in the degrees of soul-selling, be it drug dealing or preaching. So, there is no difference between selling your soul (meaning true self and true purpose) to be a world-famous anything versus a common street criminal, if you are operating outside of your God-given design and purpose. All of us were created with a unique set of characteristics, gifts, talents, and abilities that were given to us to fulfill God's Divine purpose, crafted specifically for us.

Psalm 37:4 says, "Delight yourself in the Lord, and he will give you the desires of your heart." The desires this verse speaks of are the desires that GOD places there. That is why, as you surrender your will and way to God, you may begin to desire some things that you never thought about, or even saw growing up. You may have no idea why you now want things that you either never wanted, were totally against, or never appeared to be obtainable. But, you will have a desire and boldness about pursuing them because God placed them there, and your desire will be to live a life that glorifies Him in every way.

I would also like to advise that Divine surrender is not a one-time event. Again– not salvation, but submission of your carnal nature that requires coming before God daily, acknowledging your need to lay your heart before Him in submission to His will, and total dependence on

Him. In doing so, you are affirming that it is not your will but His will, not your way but His way, and not your time but His time. Doing this as part of your daily spiritual practice invites God to take a front-row seat in your life. It also prevents your carnal mind from rising up and taking the lead on decisions concerning challenges, opportunities, and ideas that must be brought before the throne of God for His input. Liken it to an organ transplant patient taking anti-rejection drugs to ensure their new organ works efficiently in their old body. In the same way, a spiritual heart transplant requires taking spiritual anti-rejection medication, by seeking God's input on EVERYTHING, daily — through prayer, bible study, and speaking His word.

In consideration of this reflection's opening verse and all that followed, surrendering one's self might seem like an impossible task. However, I'd like to encourage you by highlighting the fact that all you're being asked to do is surrender, while God does the rest. Matthew 11:28-30 reads:

> Come to Me, all who are weary and heavy-laden, and I will give you rest. 29 Take My yoke upon you and learn from Me, for I am gentle and humble in heart, and you will find rest for your souls. 30 For My yoke is easy, and My burden is light. NASB

So, clear as day, we see that the taking up of your cross is simply taking up God's purpose for your life, endeavoring to learn of Him and live for Him in the process. In doing so, He promises that the weight of what He's called you to do will be light, and your soul will be at rest because it will be operating in harmony with the person and purpose to which He's called you. You won't be trying to figure out who and how to be when you commit to being who He called you to be. You won't have to worry about trying to fit into certain groups or conform to social and organizational expectations that are contrary to God's purpose for your life. And you will rest in knowing that because you have surrendered to the person and path to which He's called you, every need and righteous desire of your heart will be fulfilled. Through a totally surrendered person, God will perform the supernatural, as He promised that His strength is made perfect in weakness (2 Corinthians 2:9); meaning, absence of the influence of one's carnal will and way.

Although God promised that taking on the load of His purpose for your life would be easy, He didn't promise that it would be easy to wait on Him when in need, trust in Him with all your heart under pressure, and stand up to people and institutions who challenge your resolve to follow Him. Thankfully, God's word tells us over and over that all we need to do is stand in His purpose, and He will do all the defending.

I, therefore, pray that at minimum, this reflection gives you something to think about, but ultimately encourages you to go before God concerning your life. Even if you *think* you're on track, the only way to *know* is to formally surrender yourself and your plans for His review. That is the only way to ensure they align with His pre-ordained marching orders for your life, to produce the highest expression of your Divine Self in the earth. For His glory, your good, and the good of others. And it is so!

Surrender (God's Will and Way)

"If you love me, you will keep my commandments." John 14:15

And calling the crowd to him with his disciples, he said to them, If anyone would come after me, let him deny himself and take up his cross and follow me. For whoever would save his life will lose it, but whoever loses his life for my sake, and the gospel's will save it. Mark 8:34-35

And going a little farther, he fell on the ground and prayed that, if it were possible, the hour might pass from him. And he said, "Abba, Father, all things are possible for you. Remove this cup from me. Yet not what I will, but what you will." Mark 14:35-36

And he said to all, If anyone would come after me, let him deny himself and take up his cross daily and follow me. For whoever would save his life will lose it, but whoever loses his life for my sake will save it. Luke 9: 23-24

I appeal to you; therefore, brothers, by the mercies of God, to present your bodies as a living sacrifice, holy and acceptable to God, which is your spiritual worship. Do not be conformed to this world, but be transformed by the renewal of your mind, that by testing you may discern what is the will of God, what is good and acceptable and perfect. Romans 12:1-2

Let us draw near with a true heart in full assurance of faith, with our hearts sprinkled clean from an evil conscience, and our bodies washed with pure water. Let us hold fast the confession of our hope without wavering, for he who promised is faithful. Hebrews 10:22-23

But be doers of the word, and not hearers only, deceiving yourselves. James 1:22

Humble yourselves, therefore, under the mighty hand of God so that at the proper time, he may exalt you, casting all your anxieties on him, because he cares for you. Be sober-minded; be watchful. Your adversary, the devil, prowls around like a roaring lion, seeking someone to devour.

147

Resist him, firm in your faith, knowing that the same kinds of suffering are being experienced by your brotherhood throughout the world. And after you have suffered a little while, the God of all grace, who has called you to his eternal glory in Christ, will himself restore, confirm, strengthen, and establish you. 1 Peter 5:6-10

Temptation

Watch and pray that you may not enter into temptation. The spirit indeed is willing, but the flesh is weak. Matthew 26:41

Do not be overcome by evil, but overcome evil with good. Romans 12:21

No temptation has overtaken you that is not common to man. God is faithful, and he will not let you be tempted beyond your ability, but with the temptation, he will also provide the way of escape, that you may be able to endure it. 1 Corinthians 10:13

But I say, walk by the Spirit, and you will not gratify the desires of the flesh. For the desires of the flesh are against the Spirit, and the desires of the Spirit are against the flesh, for these are opposed to each other, to keep you from doing the things you want to do. Galatians 5:16-17

Brothers, if anyone is caught in any transgression, you who are spiritual should restore him in a spirit of gentleness. Keep watch on yourself, lest you too be tempted. Galatians 6:1

But those who desire to be rich fall into temptation, into a snare, into many senseless and harmful desires that plunge people into ruin and destruction. 1 Timothy 6:9

For because he himself has suffered when tempted, he is able to help those who are being tempted. Hebrews 2:18

For we do not have a high priest who is unable to sympathize with our weaknesses, but one who in every respect has been tempted as we are, yet without sin. Hebrews 4:15

Count it all joy, my brothers, when you meet trials of various kinds, for you know that the testing of your faith produces steadfastness. And let steadfastness have its full effect, that you may be perfect and complete, lacking in nothing. James 1:2-4

Blessed is the man who remains steadfast under trial, for when he has stood the test, he will receive the crown of life, which God has promised to those who love him. Let no one say when he is tempted, "I am being tempted by God," for God cannot be tempted with evil, and he himself tempts no one. But each person is tempted when he is lured and enticed by his own desire. Then desire when it has conceived gives birth to sin, and sin, when it is fully grown, brings forth death. Do not be deceived, my beloved brothers.. James 1:12-16

Submit yourselves therefore to God. Resist the devil, and he will flee from you. James 4:7

Beloved, do not be surprised at the fiery trial when it comes upon you to test you, as though something strange were happening to you.
1 Peter 4:12

Trust

And those who know your name put their trust in you, for you, O Lord, have not forsaken those who seek you. Psalm 9:10

"Be still, and know that I am God. I will be exalted among the nations, I will be exalted in the earth!" Psalm 46:10

Commit your way to the Lord; trust in him, and he will act. Psalm 37:5

Blessed is the man who makes the Lord his trust, who does not turn to the proud, to those who go astray after a lie! Psalm 40:4

Trust in him at all times, O people; pour out your heart before him; God is a refuge for us. Selah Psalm 62:8

Trust in the Lord with all your heart, and do not lean on your own understanding. In all your ways, acknowledge him, and he will make straight your paths. Proverbs 3:5-6

You keep him in perfect peace whose mind is stayed on you, because he trusts in you. Trust in the Lord forever, for the Lord God is an everlasting rock. Isaiah 26:3-4

Thus says the Lord: "Cursed is the man who trusts in man and makes flesh his strength, whose heart turns away from the Lord." Jeremiah 17:5

"Blessed is the man who trusts in the Lord, whose trust is the Lord. He is like a tree planted by water, that sends out its roots by the stream, and does not fear when heat comes, for its leaves remain green, and is not anxious in the year of drought, for it does not cease to bear fruit." Jeremiah 17:7-8

Truth

Teach me your way, O Lord, that I may walk in your truth; unite my heart to fear your name. Psalm 86:11

The Lord is near to all who call on him, to all who call on him in truth. Psalm 145:18

So Jesus said to the Jews who had believed in him, "If you abide in my word, you are truly my disciples, and you will know the truth, and the truth will set you free." John 8:31-32

When the Spirit of truth comes, he will guide you into all the truth, for he will not speak on his own authority, but whatever he hears he will speak, and he will declare to you the things that are to come. John 16:13

Rather, speaking the truth in love, we are to grow up in every way into him who is the head, into Christ, Ephesians 4:15

Therefore, having put away falsehood, let each one of you speak the truth with his neighbor, for we are members one of another. Ephesians 4:25

Victory

"The Lord will fight for you, and you have only to be silent."
Exodus 14:14

For the Lord your God is he who goes with you to fight for you against your enemies, to give you the victory. Deuteronomy 20:4

For the righteous falls seven times and rises again, but the wicked stumble in times of calamity. Proverbs 24:16

There is therefore now no condemnation for those who are in Christ Jesus. Romans 8:1

No, in all these things we are more than conquerors through him who loved us. Romans 8:37

But thanks be to God, who gives us the victory through our Lord Jesus Christ. Therefore, my beloved brothers, be steadfast, immovable, always abounding in the work of the Lord, knowing that in the Lord your labor is not in vain. 1 Corinthians 15:57-58

For the weapons of our warfare are not of the flesh but have Divine power to destroy strongholds. 2 Corinthians 10:4

For God gave us a spirit not of fear but of power and love and self-control. 2 Timothy 1:7

For everyone who has been born of God overcomes the world. And this is the victory that has overcome the world—our faith. 1 John 5:4

Vision – Plans/Goals

Without counsel plans fail, but with many advisers they succeed. Proverbs 15:22

Commit your work to the Lord, and your plans will be established. Proverbs 16:3

The heart of man plans his way, but the Lord establishes his steps. Proverbs 16:9

Where there is no prophetic vision the people cast off restraint, but blessed is he who keeps the law. Proverbs 29:18

For I know the plans I have for you, declares the Lord, plans for welfare and not for evil, to give you a future and a hope. Jeremiah 29:11

And the Lord answered me: "Write the vision; make it plain on tablets, so he may run who reads it. For still the vision awaits its appointed time; it hastens to the end—it will not lie. If it seems slow, wait for it; it will surely come; it will not delay. Habakkuk 2:2-3

Voice of God (Was that You God?)

All Scripture is breathed out by God and profitable for teaching, for reproof, for correction, and for training in righteousness, that the man of God may be competent, equipped for every good work.
2 Timothy 3:16-17

Therefore, just as the Holy Spirit says, "Today if you hear His voice, Do not harden your hearts (Hebrews 3:7-8), we must endeavor to learn the voice of God through reading His word, be willing and available to follow His leading, and be equipped to stand against deceiving spirits by speaking the word in opposition to ungodly influences.

How to Know the Difference between the Lord's voice, and other voices.

Adapted from The Scripture Keys for Kingdom Living – June Newman Davis

John 10:3, 5, 27
3 To him the doorkeeper opens, and the sheep hear his voice, and he calls his own sheep by name and leads them out. . . . 5 A stranger they simply will not follow, but will flee from him, because they do not know the voice of strangers. 27 My sheep hear My voice, and I know them, and they follow Me;

John 18:37

Therefore Pilate said to Him, "So You are a king?" Jesus answered, "You say correctly that I am a king. For this I have been born, and for this I have come into the world, to testify to the truth. Everyone who is of the truth hears My voice."

1 Corinthians 12:3

Therefore I make known to you that no one speaking by the Spirit of God says, "Jesus is accursed"; and no one can say, "Jesus is Lord," except by the Holy Spirit.

<u>**WHEN THE LORD SPEAKS,**</u> the following is evident:

AN INWARD KNOWING – Sometimes, He speaks words that are not familiar or common to your vocabulary. – 1 Corinthians 2:13
PEACE – fills your soul, and you are at rest. – John 14:27
CONFIDENCE – in His provided instruction follows. – Isaiah 30:15
AGREEMENT WITH GOD'S WORD – the Bible. God will not violate His word, so you MUST check with the Bible (II Peter 1:19).
CONFIRMATION – God always confirms His word to you, especially in guidance for action (II Corinthians 13:1)

<u>**WHEN SATAN OR ANOTHER EVIL SPIRIT SPEAKS,**</u> the following is evident:

DOUBT, FEAR, DISCOMFORT – (II Timothy 1:7, Romans 8:15-16)
CONFLICT, RESTLESSNESS, NO PEACE – (Jas. 3:14-18, Isa. 48:22)
QUESTIONING, WONDERING – If it is God (Romans 14:23)
CONFUSION – If you have to "work it out," forget it! God's will is clear. Satan is the "author of confusion." (Jas. 3:16, 1 Cor. 14:33)

OPPOSITION TO GOD'S LEADING/COMMAND – to us personally or through scripture. When God speaks, Satan soon says the exact opposite, trying to snatch away the Word (Matthew 13:4, 18, 24-30, Genesis 3:4)
CONDEMNATION, GUILT, DISCOURAGEMENT – Satan brings up sins that have already been confessed, forgiven, and forgotten by God (Romans 8:1, John 3:20, Revelation 12:10)

WHEN THE CARNAL/FLESH-SELF SPEAKS,
the following is evident:

HESITATION–Self has to think before it speaks, God's Word to us flows easily without any preconceptions due to our carnal mind (Romans 8:5-7; cp. 26-27)

DECEPTION – We can be led astray by our own hearts, since we do not fully understand ourselves (Jeremiah 17:9-10). So, we must feed on the Word until we become mature (Hebrews 5:12).

DOUBLE-MINDEDNESS – Wanting two opposite things at the same time results in instability (James 1:8). Jesus gives us the "single eye" (Matthew 6:22-23) that chooses the Kingdom first (Matthew 6:33) so that we can really want to do God's will (Philippians 2:13). It is the indwelling Spirit that enables us to do this (John 14:16, 16:13).

UNREGENERATE DESIRES – The voice sounds like our own, with our own inflections and intentions, and speaks of the same old desires that you used to indulge in (James 14:16). Such desires arise from the flesh, and we must consider ourselves dead to those desires (Romans 6:1-4).

Waiting on God

I believe that I shall look upon the goodness of the Lord in the land of the living! Wait for the Lord; be strong, and let your heart take courage; wait for the Lord! Psalm 27:13-14

Therefore the Lord waits to be gracious to you, and therefore he exalts himself to show mercy to you. For the Lord is a God of justice; blessed are all those who wait for him. Isaiah 30:18

The Lord is good to those who wait for him, to the soul who seeks him. Lamentations 3:25

But as for me, I will look to the Lord; I will wait for the God of my salvation; my God will hear me. Micah 7:7

And let us not grow weary of doing good, for in due season we will reap, if we do not give up. Galatians 6:9

Blessed is the man who remains steadfast under trial, for when he has stood the test, he will receive the crown of life, which God has promised to those who love him. James 1:12

Wisdom

So teach us to number our days that we may get a heart of wisdom. Psalm 90:12

The fear of the Lord is the beginning of wisdom; all those who practice it have a good understanding. His praise endures forever! Psalm 111:10

Blessed is the one who finds wisdom, and the one who gets understanding, for the gain from her is better than gain from silver and her profit better than gold. She is more precious than jewels, and nothing you desire can compare with her. Long life is in her right hand; in her left hand are riches and honor. Her ways are ways of pleasantness, and all her paths are peace. Proverbs 3:13-18

The way of a fool is right in his own eyes, but a wise man listens to advice. Proverbs 12:15

For the protection of wisdom is like the protection of money, and the advantage of knowledge is that wisdom preserves the life of him who has it. Ecclesiastes 7:12

For I will give you a mouth and wisdom, which none of your adversaries will be able to withstand or contradict. Luke 21:15

If any of you lacks wisdom, let him ask God, who gives generously to all without reproach, and it will be given him. James 1:5

Who is wise and understanding among you? By his good conduct let him show his works in the meekness of wisdom. James 3:13

But the wisdom from above is first pure, then peaceable, gentle, open to reason, full of mercy and good fruits, impartial and sincere. James 3:17

Let the word of Christ dwell in you richly, teaching and admonishing one another in all wisdom, singing psalms and hymns and spiritual songs, with thankfulness in your hearts to God. Colossians 3:16

Walk in wisdom toward outsiders, making the best use of the time. Let your speech always be gracious, seasoned with salt, so that you may know how you ought to answer each person. Colossians 4:5-6

Reflections on Divine Self-worth (Identity)

Although this reflection is at the end of the book, I believe it is one of the most important sections. The reason being, that it has been proven time and again in my life and in the lives of many others, that unless one commits to something with an inward motivation, it is unlikely they will stick to it. The same can be said for making a commitment to follow God and surrendering your natural self to live according to the highest (Divine) form of your existence.

However, I personally don't believe that one can embark on that journey until they have taken the time to learn who they are, what they have to offer to this world, and, thus, where they are going. I am not talking about observing an admirable life goal, profession, or ideal and striving to emulate it. I'm talking about placing yourself before the Father, you know, your Creator. Asking him to show you who you are, in HIM, and then asking Him how you should go about living according to the standard that befits your royal status.

Royalty doesn't just "hang out" with anyone. Royalty doesn't just eat any ol' thing, or go to unsavory places. Royalty has a certain kind of walk, talk, and disposition. Royalty presents a certain poise that only comes about through a firm grounding in the knowledge of their royal status and the power that status effectuates in the world. But even the Queen of England had to be groomed. Even though she was royalty from birth, she still had to be taught how to be "Royalty."

Who else can better teach you how to walk in power, yet quiet strength, grace, poise, and all things Royal than the King of Kings and Lord of Lords Himself? Quite frankly, no one. So, it amazes me how we, as God's creation, continue to look to other people, social media, TV, and even religious tradition (different from Biblical teaching), to show us how to "Be." And I believe therein lies the root cause of so many people being imprisoned by the personas they construct and the high sense of self-esteem they project as a result of their accomplishments, and/or how other people perceive the image they project.

Healthyplace.com defines healthy self-esteem as:
- The manner in which we evaluate ourselves. It is our internal assessment of our qualities and attributes. We have healthy self-esteem when what we think, feel, and believe about ourselves is honest and realistic.

On the contrary, it defines unhealthy self-esteem as either too high:
- When you exaggerate your positive traits or deceive yourself about your faults and weaknesses, or lead you to fall into the trap of narcissism, where you believe you are superior in one way or another over others.

Or too low:
- When you underestimate – or flat out ignore – your positive characteristics. People with low self-esteem also tend to view themselves through a harsh and negative filter.

They then went on to define self-worth as the belief that you are loveable and valuable regardless of how you and/or others evaluate your traits.

I listed their definition because it was one of the most concise I found, and ties into my follow-up question to address this common issue among so many people. Ready? Here it goes:

How do you know that you are loved, valued, and WORTHY just for who you are, and not because of your accomplishments, appearance, talents, etc. if you haven't been taught what true inner self-worth is? Where does your identity come from if you haven't been raised to affirm that you are loved and valuable just for being you, because God created you, and you therefore have a Divine purpose in Him? I've found that many people don't know. At least I didn't, and after almost forty years, I am just finding out. How do people have thriving relationships and successful careers where they are truly giving of their gifts, talents, and abilities, and not just increasing in title and salary, when they don't truly know who they are, and why they were created?

I felt it was important to add this to the book, in hopes that the steps I took to learn how to walk in my true, Divine Identity, can help someone discover theirs. So here's what I did, and not of my own volition, but through a series of events, circumstances, and suffering that made me stop and evaluate the need for change.

Helpful Steps to Understanding Your Divine Worth

1) Memorize and speak God's word and affirmations concerning your Divine worth. I've listed a number of scriptures below, and a few affirmations following that. Affirm your Divine worth and value that was attributed to you at birth and, thus, was no act of your own. It can, therefore, never be taken or lost, just diminished when you live your life in ways that ignore or abort the Royal standard by which you've been made to uphold.

2) Ask God to reveal anything and anyone in your life that you are currently engaged, committed, and/or otherwise not Divinely designed to be connected to, and either remove them from your path or bring them into harmony with your Divine self, as you surrender to His Divine plan.

160

3) Daily, in word and deed, surrender your heart to the Father to be used as a vessel for His glory. That doesn't mean you have to start preaching sermons or laying hands on people in the supermarket. You can be a light in this world on your current job, in your current community, or any other place God places you. The key is to maintain a heart that is open and available to be led by the Spirit of God each day. Not my will, but Thy will. Not my way, but Thy way. Not my time, but Thy time. And in the twinkling of an eye, it is done. You can do this by praying that desire daily, and even during times you are faced with decisions concerning God's path for your life.

4) Be willing to say "yes" to opportunities to serve and give of your gifts, talents, and abilities in ways that you would have never considered when you were living life on your terms. The same goes for saying "no" to things that would fit your self-made persona, or you know would provide you with more wealth, status, accolades, or whatever - IF - it does not fit the new path in which God seems to be leading you.

When I first committed to surrendering my life to God, not accepting Christ, because I had already done that. But really surrendering my life, my plans, and my way to God, I gave Him an unequivocal "yes". Meaning– if I was asked to serve in any way, I did so to the best of my ability, unto the Lord. I did not fully commit to an auxiliary or function full-time, because God had not yet confirmed my assignment. However, if I was available, I would serve, and if I felt God leading me to step back, I respectfully declined. When God was ready to transition me to my actual assignment, He provided the pause and pathway for transition. During that season, I learned to seek Him in everything because I was in unchartered waters. I also learned to wait on Him and stand firm in what

I was assigned to do because I KNEW it was a task, assignment, or lesson that was essential to the next season of my life.

This was my path. However, if you haven't already done so, I encourage you to take a moment and inquire about God's will for your life. Open your heart before him and be willing to yield to His leading concerning the person He would have you be, and path He would have you take; for His Glory, your good, and the good of others. And it is so!

Worth - Divine Worth in God

So God created man in his own image, in the image of God, he created him; male and female he created them. Genesis 1:27

For you formed my inward parts; you knitted me together in my mother's womb. I praise you, for I am fearfully and wonderfully made. Wonderful are your works; my soul knows it very well. My frame was not hidden from you when I was being made in secret, intricately woven in the depths of the earth. Your eyes saw my unformed substance; in your book were written, every one of them, the days that were formed for me, when as yet there was none of them. Psalm 139:13-16

Because you are precious in my eyes and honored, and I love you, I give men in return for you, peoples in exchange for your life. Isaiah 43:4

Are not five sparrows sold for two pennies? And not one of them is forgotten before God. Why, even the hairs of your head are all numbered. Fear not; you are of more value than many sparrows.
Luke 12:6-7

For while we were still weak, at the right time Christ died for the ungodly. For one will scarcely die for a righteous person—though perhaps for a good person one would dare even to die— but God shows his love for us in that while we were still sinners, Christ died for us. Romans 5:6-8

Even as he chose us in him before the foundation of the world, that we should be holy and blameless before him in love: Ephesians 1:4

You did not choose me, but I chose you and appointed you that you should go and bear fruit and that your fruit should abide, so that whatever you ask the Father in my name, he may give it to you. John 15:16

But you are a chosen race, a royal priesthood, a holy nation, a people for his own possession, that you may proclaim the excellencies of him who called you out of darkness into his marvelous light. 1 Peter 2:9

Affirmations for Divine Self Worth

I believe in God. He is my Father. He loves me, and I love Him. He dwells in me, and I in Him, and therefore, I am a reflection of his love, life, and light in this world.

I now smash and demolish by my spoken word, every untrue record of my subconscious mind. They shall return to the dust heap of their native nothingness, for they came from my own vain imaginations. I now make new records through the Christ within; the records of health, wealth, love, and perfect self-expression.

Father, I thank you that I am whole and complete and that I and all my affairs are in Divine order; my health, my finances, my perfect work, my family, and all my relationships.

I thank you that in reflecting your love, light, and life, I am always kind, patient, loving, joyful, humble, poised, gentle, and meek in every situation. I think and believe the best of everyone and greet everyone with a warm smile and a cheerful greeting – through the power and assistance of the Holy Spirit – moment-by-moment, day-by-day.

I dissolve in my own mind and the mind of all others, any idea that my own good can be withheld from me. That which is for my highest good now comes to me through God's grace, and I welcome it.

The power of God is working through me, to free me of every negative influence. All power is given unto me for good, in my mind, body, and affairs – and I rightly use it now!

Prayer Journal

Therefore, confess your sins to one another, and pray for one another so that you may be healed. The effective prayer of a righteous man can accomplish much. James 5:16 NASB

Prayer Request   Name: _____   Date: _____

_____

_____

_____

_____

_____

_____

_____

Prayer Request   Name: _____   Date: _____

_____

_____

_____

_____

_____

_____

_____

Praise   *Rejoice always, pray without ceasing, give thanks in all circumstances; for this is the will of God in Christ Jesus for you. 1 Thessalonians 5:16-18 ESV*

_____

_____

_____

_____

_____

_____

_____

Prayer Journal

Therefore, confess your sins to one another, and pray for one another so that you may be healed. The effective prayer of a righteous man can accomplish much. James 5:16 NASB

Prayer Request   Name: _____   Date: _____

_____
_____
_____
_____
_____
_____
_____
_____

Prayer Request   Name: _____   Date: _____

_____
_____
_____
_____
_____
_____
_____
_____

Praise   *Rejoice always, pray without ceasing, give thanks in all circumstances; for this is the will of God in Christ Jesus for you. 1 Thessalonians 5:16-18 ESV*

_____
_____
_____
_____
_____
_____
_____

Prayer Journal

Therefore, confess your sins to one another, and pray for one another so that you may be healed.
The effective prayer of a righteous man can accomplish much. James 5:16 NASB

Prayer Request   Name: _____   Date: _____

_____

_____

_____

_____

_____

_____

_____

Prayer Request   Name: _____   Date: _____

_____

_____

_____

_____

_____

_____

_____

Praise   *Rejoice always, pray without ceasing, give thanks in all circumstances;*
for this is the will of God in Christ Jesus for you. 1 Thessalonians 5:16-18 ESV

_____

_____

_____

_____

_____

_____

_____

Prayer Journal

Therefore, confess your sins to one another, and pray for one another so that you may be healed.
The effective prayer of a righteous man can accomplish much. James 5:16 NASB

Prayer Request   Name: _____   Date: _____

_____
_____
_____
_____
_____
_____
_____

Prayer Request   Name: _____   Date: _____

_____
_____
_____
_____
_____
_____
_____

Praise   *Rejoice always, pray without ceasing, give thanks in all circumstances;*
for this is the will of God in Christ Jesus for you. 1 Thessalonians 5:16-18 ESV

_____
_____
_____
_____
_____
_____

Prayer Journal

Therefore, confess your sins to one another, and pray for one another so that you may be healed.
The effective prayer of a righteous man can accomplish much. James 5:16 NASB

Prayer Request   Name: _____   Date: _____

_____
_____
_____
_____
_____
_____
_____

Prayer Request   Name: _____   Date: _____

_____
_____
_____
_____
_____
_____
_____

Praise

Rejoice always, pray without ceasing, give thanks in all circumstances;
for this is the will of God in Christ Jesus for you. 1 Thessalonians 5:16-18 ESV

_____
_____
_____
_____
_____
_____
_____

Prayer Journal

Therefore, confess your sins to one another, and pray for one another so that you may be healed. The effective prayer of a righteous man can accomplish much. James 5:16 NASB

Prayer Request   Name: _____   Date: _____

_____
_____
_____
_____
_____
_____
_____

Prayer Request   Name: _____   Date: _____

_____
_____
_____
_____
_____
_____
_____

Praise

Rejoice always, pray without ceasing, give thanks in all circumstances; for this is the will of God in Christ Jesus for you. 1 Thessalonians 5:16-18 ESV

_____
_____
_____
_____
_____
_____
_____

Prayer Journal

Therefore, confess your sins to one another, and pray for one another so that you may be healed.
The effective prayer of a righteous man can accomplish much. James 5:16 NASB

Prayer Request   Name: _____   Date: _____

_____

_____

_____

_____

_____

_____

_____

_____

Prayer Request   Name: _____   Date: _____

_____

_____

_____

_____

_____

_____

_____

_____

Praise   Rejoice always, pray without ceasing, give thanks in all circumstances;
          for this is the will of God in Christ Jesus for you. 1 Thessalonians 5:16-18 ESV

_____

_____

_____

_____

_____

_____

_____

Prayer Journal

Therefore, confess your sins to one another, and pray for one another so that you may be healed.
The effective prayer of a righteous man can accomplish much. James 5:16 NASB

Prayer Request   Name: _____   Date: _____

_____

_____

_____

_____

_____

_____

_____

Prayer Request   Name: _____   Date: _____

_____

_____

_____

_____

_____

_____

_____

Praise   *Rejoice always, pray without ceasing, give thanks in all circumstances;*
for this is the will of God in Christ Jesus for you. 1 Thessalonians 5:16-18 ESV

_____

_____

_____

_____

_____

_____

_____

Prayer Journal

Therefore, confess your sins to one another, and pray for one another so that you may be healed.
The effective prayer of a righteous man can accomplish much. James 5:16 NASB

Prayer Request   Name: _____   Date: _____

_____

_____

_____

_____

_____

_____

_____

Prayer Request   Name: _____   Date: _____

_____

_____

_____

_____

_____

_____

_____

Praise   *Rejoice always, pray without ceasing, give thanks in all circumstances;*
for this is the will of God in Christ Jesus for you. 1 Thessalonians 5:16-18 ESV

_____

_____

_____

_____

_____

_____

_____

Prayer Journal

Therefore, confess your sins to one another, and pray for one another so that you may be healed.
The effective prayer of a righteous man can accomplish much. James 5:16 NASB

Prayer Request Name: _____ Date: _____

_____
_____
_____
_____
_____
_____
_____
_____

Prayer Request Name: _____ Date: _____

_____
_____
_____
_____
_____
_____
_____
_____

Praise

Rejoice always, pray without ceasing, give thanks in all circumstances;
for this is the will of God in Christ Jesus for you. 1 Thessalonians 5:16-18 ESV

_____
_____
_____
_____
_____
_____
_____

Prayer Journal

Therefore, confess your sins to one another, and pray for one another so that you may be healed.
The effective prayer of a righteous man can accomplish much. James 5:16 NASB

Prayer Request   Name: _____   Date: _____

_____
_____
_____
_____
_____
_____
_____
_____

Prayer Request   Name: _____   Date: _____

_____
_____
_____
_____
_____
_____
_____

Praise   *Rejoice always, pray without ceasing, give thanks in all circumstances;*
for this is the will of God in Christ Jesus for you. 1 Thessalonians 5:16-18 ESV

_____
_____
_____
_____
_____
_____
_____

J. MARIE is a mom to a wildly talented little girl, bursting with life and comedic energy. She is also a former media professional, who traded in her role in the areas of video production and communications, to walk in her God-ordained role of daughter and dedicated follower of the Most-High. Her passion is sharing with others the wonders and peace that follow those who accept Jesus Christ as their savior. She desires to be a sister and guide to the believer, dispatched by the Father to assist those endeavoring to be transformed into His image, through the spiritual practice of internalizing God's word and engaging in the daily discipline of affirming it in their lives.